WORDS
OF HOPE

in the Midst of Lou Gehrig's Disease

By Pastor Donald L. Roberts

Minnesota Heritage Publishing
2008

For more information, contact:
Minnesota Heritage Publishing
205 Ledlie Lane, Suite 125
Mankato, MN 56001
www.mnheritage.com

ISBN: 978-0-9794940-3-1

Library of Congress Catalog Number: 2008939097

Published by Minnesota Heritage Publishing

Printed in the United States of America
By Corporate Graphics, North Mankato, MN

First Edition

Dedication

Dedicated to the people of Emmanuel Lutheran Church where I grew up and the people of East and West Sveadahl Lutheran Churches of St. James, First Lutheran Church of Red Wing, and Bethlehem Lutheran Church of Mankato, all of which I was privileged to serve as pastor. These people helped me grow in faith.

Acknowledgments

I would like to thank Pastor Dennis Peterson, pastor of Emmanuel Lutheran Church in Two Harbors, MN, my sister, Betty, the people of Bethlehem Lutheran Church, and my wife, Bonnie, for encouraging me to publish these devotions. I would also like to thank my wife and my nurses, Pam Miller and Lori Steen, for holding the letter board while I dictated these devotions. Most of all, I want to thank my family for not giving up on me during my struggle with Lou Gehrig's Disease. They struggled too.

Table of Contents

                                                                    Page

Foreword i

Renewal. 1

Look to the Past 2

Undefeated People of God 3

Fear Toward Hope. 4

Praise, Sovereignty, and the Poor and Needy 5

Look to the Future 7

Trust God 8

The Essence of Faith 9

Intergenerational Sharing 10

Dependence on God 11

Jesus Isn't the Reason: He Is the Answer 12

A Brighter Day 13

God's Call 15

Doubt 16

Chosen by God 17

Exile Experiences 18

Interdependent People. 19

Life's Unfairness 20

Wonderful Works of God 21

Emptying Oneself 22

A Place for You 23

Theological Struggles. 24

Born Again, and Again 26

Grace. 27

Pray, Trust, Praise 28

A Tent vs. A House 29

Places of God's Presence 30

In Christ, We are Strong. 31

The Treasure of Christ 32

Individualism vs. Christian Identity 33

Our Source of Help. 34

We Need Each Other 35

Evangelism and Social Ministry 36

A Repeat 37

Praise God 38

Prayer – Communication with God. 39

God's Will Prevails 40

Jesus Strengthens Us 41

Suffering to Hope 42

Reasons for Thankfulness 43

God's Silence 44

God's Possessions 45

Worship and Education 46

God Knows Us 47

Where Can I Go From Your Presence?. 48

The Word Became Flesh. 49

Patience 50

Dynamics of the Church 51

Amazing Grace 52

Mighty Acts of God 53

Resurrection. 54

Fear to Hope 55

Public Officials 56

You Can Do It. 57

The Reason We Were Created. 58

Consolation 59
Origins of Faith. 60
Christmas Equals the Cross 61
A New Beginning 62
Patience Through Suffering. 63
God's Kingdom is Near 64
The Reality of Sin 65
Steadfastness. 66
Testing Our Faith 67
Hope in Clay Jars 68
Our Need for Jesus 69
The Silence of God 70
The Means of Grace 71
Closer to Jesus 72
Pray Without Ceasing 73
Raised with Christ. 74
My Yoke is Easy. 75
The Value of Trust 76
God With Us 77
Forgiveness. 78
Thankfulness in all Circumstances 79
Thankfulness for People. 80
Be Like a Child 81
Hope Through Suffering. 82
When 'In Sickness and Health' Becomes a Reality 85
    By Bonnie L. Roberts
Living With ALS - A Daughter's Perspective 91
    By Katie J. Roberts

Foreword

"Those symptoms definitely indicate ALS (Amyotrophic Lateral Sclerosis, or the more common name, Lou Gehrig's Disease)." Those were the words of a neurologist on September 9th, 1995.

I grew up in Two Harbors, Minnesota. I came from a loving family, a family of four. A particular joy was grouse hunting with my dad or friends. In high school, I was active in cross country, swimming, and track. I was a mediocre athlete, but enjoyed the involvement. It is important to note that this involvement contributed to a lifestyle where, except for a few years, swimming and jogging were an integral part of my life.

Pastor Donald L. Roberts
(taken one year after ALS diagnosis, 1996)

I attended the University of Minnesota, Duluth, majoring in business administration. All the while I was thinking about becoming a pastor, but was unsure of taking this direction. What convinced me was when I was interviewing for business positions. Though some seemed appealing, they didn't seem right for me. I came to see that as God's call to become a pastor. I have now been a pastor of the Evangelical Lutheran Church in America and one of its predecessor bodies for thirty-two years.

I first felt symptoms in May of 1995, but easily dismissed them as some sort of minor physical oddity. As symptoms progressed, I began to wonder about ALS. Though ALS symptoms can occur in various places of the body, mine were loss of partial control of two fingers in my left hand. Gradually, it progressed to my whole left hand. In time, I experienced quivering in my left arm. A word of caution: Many minor physical problems can mimic ALS. If you experience these symptoms, it might not necessarily be ALS. I knew the symptoms of ALS from a former parishioner who developed the disease in 1986. The whole congregation, and I as pastor, witnessed the devastating effects of ALS on this man. I consulted with a medical encyclopedia. The symptoms I had were a text book case of ALS. By July of that summer, I was scared. I plodded, or more accurately endured, the rest of the summer. I tried to minister to people, but the specter of ALS haunted me. As a form of denial, I visited a chiropractor. Certainly I wanted it to be something spinal that could be corrected by the manipulations they do. After the initial visit, I was fearfully hopeful. As symptoms progressed, I asked for a referral to a neurologist.

While I was diagnosed in 1995, I worked as a pastor through December 31, 1996. 1996 began with only minor symptoms. The symptoms I experienced had no detrimental effect on my work. As the year progressed, so did my symptoms. I began to have trouble walking and speaking. Gradually my pastoral colleague assumed a greater share of the work. Finally, with the encouragement of my bishop, I resigned due to health reasons. From the end of 1996 until 2000 my symptoms continued to increase, going from using a cane to using a walker and finally a wheelchair. My voice also deteriorated. I went from most people being able to understand me to only my wife, Bonnie, being able to understand me. Gradually I had to use a transparent letter board. On the letter board are the letters and numbers. My eyes point to the desired letter or number. In this way I spell words. It is a painstakingly slow process. To this day, it is how I perform verbal and written communication. On the lighter side, this type of communication has advantages for my wife. When she and I have arguments, she simply removes the board, leaving me speechless.

There are many misconceptions about ALS. Unlike spinal chord injuries, ALS doesn't affect one's tactile sense. ALS only affects movements, not the ability to feel. Also ALS doesn't affect the ability to hear or see. Because I can't speak, and am in a wheelchair, some people think they have to speak loudly and slowly. ALS also doesn't affect one's mind. Many a time I have chuckled inside when a well meaning dear friend tells me their name when I remember it well.

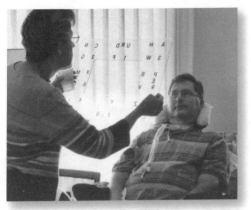

Bonnie holding the letter board while Don spells a word, one letter at a time.

One area where my ALS is different than many people's ALS is that I have retained some leg movement. A physical therapist prescribed some exercises for my legs in the hope they might strengthen. His warning was that too much exercise can have a reverse affect with ALS, so I am very cautious not to overdo the exercises. Where this will lead, I do not know, but I keep working on them.

One of the aspects of ALS is whether or not to go on a ventilator when breathing becomes impaired. I had decided not to do that, not wanting to live with the restrictions that a ventilator would entail. That all changed on the morning of May 3, 2000. I had been experiencing breathing difficulty prior to that date, but that morning I had difficulty waking up. My body was filling with carbon dioxide. That is how most ALS patients die. It is really painless. Bonnie reacted, and I was rushed to the hospital. They installed a temporary ventilator, and the neurologist who diagnosed me five years earlier asked me the question, "Do you want to go on a ventilator?" In the blink of an eye, I blinked yes. I was not ready to leave my wife and my children. While there are bad days on a ventilator, I have had many good days. We have two sons, Jeremy and Paul, and a daughter, Katie. I have seen Jeremy, Paul, and Katie graduate from high school. I have seen all three graduate from college. I have shared in the joyful wedding celebrations of both of our sons. I have heard the first cries of our first grandchild, Ethan Kyle Roberts. I was able to hold him within an hour of his birth. Nothing can compare to the joy of experiencing these special family memories.

Since I went on the ventilator seven years ago, I have been cared for by nurses and personal care attendants 19 hours each day. My family completes the other five. The nurses and personal care attendants do an excellent job. I still experience both good and bad days. While I do not know what the future holds, I do hope for a cure. All in all, I am glad I'm still here.

Jeremy K. Roberts, Katie J. Roberts, Paul K. Roberts (taken October 1, 2005 at Jeremy and Dawn's wedding)

I do not believe that God caused my ALS, nor for that matter, other tragedies that people experience. I do believe God has taught me things through ALS, though it has been painful. One aspect of what God has taught me is never

Jeremy and Dawn and Ethan Kyle Roberts (taken at Paul's wedding, June 14, 2008)

take things for granted. I used to be very active physically. A pleasure was rising at 5 o'clock and jogging several miles every other morning. I still miss that. I figured if I did that I would be graced with good health far into old age. Though I knew about ALS, the chances seemed minimal that I would develop it. That changed when I was 46 years old. I am now 58. For twelve years I have watched ALS destroy my body. What I am saying is never take good things for granted. Thank God for them.

Another thing God has taught me is to be thankful for little things. Bonnie and I used to plan trips that we would take. Now I would be thankful to visit a restaurant and eat normally (currently I am fed through a feeding tube). One's perspective changes. Now I have learned to be thankful for smaller things, such as letters, visits, or phone calls from friends. A good day is deeply appreciated. I have learned to thank God for a good blood test or an encouraging physical therapy visit. Be thankful for little things.

Never underestimate or demean yourselves as the people of God. I have gained new appreciation for Christians as the body of Christ. Many times during this illness, with its multiple frustrations and seemingly unanswered prayers, I have

wondered where God is; only to see God acting and hear God speaking through other people. I believe that God frequently speaks and acts through other people. Never underestimate yourselves.

I would like to thank the people of Bethlehem Lutheran Church in Mankato, MN, for standing with me and my family. They still do. When I

Paul and Carrie Roberts on their wedding day, June 14, 2008

informed the congregation

of my diagnosis, they were supportive in both tangible and intangible ways. I will be eternally grateful for their prayers. When my voice became unable to give a sermon, members of the congregation would speak them for me. I would write the sermon and they would speak it. When my walking became uncertain, they built railings behind our free standing altar. When my illness progressed to the point where I had to resign, they visited regularly, sent letters and cards, performed maintenance around our house, provided weekly meals, and did house cleaning for us. They still do that even though I resigned ten years ago. They have truly been the body of Christ.

I have prayed constantly for physical healing. As of this writing, that has not happened. This has been painful, extremely so. Why does God seemingly not answer our prayers? I have come to believe that it is to teach us patience. Patience is a painful quality to learn. As a child, one of my expressions was, "I hate to wait." As an adult, I haven't changed much. When it comes to health matters, I am not a patient person. Yet, patience is, I believe, necessary to our growth in Christ. God has been teaching me that, however painful it has been. It was Henri Nouwen who said, "Hope without patience is wishful thinking." I believe he was correct. God is a God of hope, but to appreciate that hope, we need patience. God teaches us patience through seemingly unanswered prayer.

The devotions that follow are those I have written for our monthly Bethlehem Lutheran Church newsletter. Some are topical, some are seasonal, and some are born out of personal struggle. Those originating from personal struggle are those which have required me to evaluate what I really believe. Why does God allow illness? Why does God seemingly not answer prayer? Where is God during trouble? These are some of the questions with which I have struggled. As you read them, you may be able to detect that struggle. It is my prayer that, whatever you are facing, these devotions are helpful to you.

Nouwen, H. (1991). Creative ministry. New York: Doubleday

WORDS OF HOPE

Renewal

"Create in me a clean heart, O God, and put a new and right spirit within me."

Psalm 51:10

Psalm 51 is historically related to Ash Wednesday, which is the beginning of lent. Its focus is spiritual renewal. The word lent comes from an old English word that means "lengthen." Lent coincides with lengthening days, thus a renewal from the drabness of winter. It is during this time that we are spiritually renewed as well.

The writer of Psalm 51 was struggling with a physical illness as verse 8 makes clear, though the main focus of the Psalm is not physical healing, but spiritual renewal. I, too, have struggled with illness. I, too, need spiritual renewal. The fact that God has not healed my illness has made me angry and, at times, bitter. In prayer I have experienced God's silence. That is frustrating. I would prefer answers rather than silence. Ironically, God works through the silence to renew our faith. It is important that we explore the silence through prayer.

What is it for you? Is it an illness that won't go away? Is it some persistent sin? Is it some obstinate world problem such as hunger, poverty, or war? When you pray about these things you might experience God's silence. Keep exploring the silence through prayer. Listen to what God is saying. The silence is frustrating, but out of the silence comes renewal.

Written February 15, 2002

Look to the Past

Read Psalm 42

The author of Psalm 42 was deeply religious; yet, for this person, things were not going well. The writer says in verse 3, "My tears have been my food day and night..." However, the writer doesn't stop there. In the next verse, the author sights past worship experiences. There is a truth here. When going through difficult times, looking at past religious experiences strengthens our faith for the present. It might be an old Sunday school song. It might be some scripture that you have memorized. It might be some time when God seemed particularly close. It might be a past worship experience. The truth is this: Looking to past religious experiences strengthens our faith for the present.

In verse 9, the author writes, "I say to God, my rock: Why hast thou forgotten me?" Throughout the book of Psalms, God is referred to as a rock. In other words, God is the writer's strength and hope. Yet, at the same time, the author feels forgotten by God. When going through difficult times, these two motifs often coincide. We acknowledge God as our hope and strength and, at the same time, feel forgotten by God. It is no sin to feel this way. Ironically, in fact, the reason we feel forgotten by God is that, down deep, God is still our strength and hope.

In verse 5 and 11, we have the refrain, which reads, "Why are you cast down, O my soul, and why are you disquieted within me? Hope in God; for I shall again praise Him, my help and my God." The resurrection of Jesus guarantees the truth of this refrain. Often, in the stress of daily living, we don't feel like praising God. For instance, when caught in traffic and late for an appointment, our first thought is not of praising God. But, on a deeper level, the resurrection keeps us going when nothing else will. Because Jesus lives, we shall again praise God. It is guaranteed.

Written March 15, 2002

Undefeated People of God

Read Romans 8:31-39

An athletic team begins the season hoping to be undefeated. There is joy when they accomplish this feat. As the people of God, we are undefeated too. The text above gives at least three reasons why this is so. Verses 31 and 32 read, "What then shall we say to this? If God is for us, who is against us? He who did not spare his own Son but gave him up for us all, will he not also give us all things with him?" God has given us a future. That is God's gift to us. Sometimes our anger at God blurs the joy of this gift. Most of us get angry with God when prayers don't seem to be answered in the desired way or when we think God doesn't act as we think God should. The anger is real. The future, which God has given, is stronger than the anger. With this future assured, we can still pray, worship, and serve.

Verse 33 and 34 say, "Who shall bring any charge against God's elect? It is God who justifies; who is to condemn? Is it Christ Jesus, who died, yes, who was raised from the dead, who is at the right hand of God, who indeed intercedes for us?" God does not condemn us; our sin does. Sin separates us from God, others, and ourselves. Sin makes us less than whole. Furthermore, we can't do anything about it. The confession we say on Sunday has it right: "We are in bondage to sin and cannot free ourselves." The good news is this: Through the death and resurrection of Jesus we are forgiven. This forgiveness is complete. It covers every sin. In the power of this forgiveness, we turn from sin and live as God wants us to live.

Verse 39 assures us that nothing can separate us from the love of God. Frequently the world makes us feel unlovable. It might come from something someone said. It might come from failure to meet personal goals. It might come from a personal problem. Remember, nothing can separate us from God who loves us. Because God loves us, we have strength to work on personal problems. We can be optimistic people. After all, because of Christ, we are undefeated.

Written April 15, 2002

Fear Toward Hope

"Then he said, 'Your name shall no more be called Jacob, but Israel, for you have striven with God and with men, and have prevailed.'"

Genesis 32:28

The verse quoted above represents a pivotal time in Jacob's life. Earlier in his life he had cheated his brother Esau out of his rightful inheritance. Now Esau was coming with four hundred men to meet Jacob. As indicated earlier in chapter 32, Jacob was afraid. In this context of fear, God wrestles with Jacob and makes of him a new person. In the Old Testament a name change signifies a change in character. The name Israel means "God rules." Jacob, in the midst of his fear, came to trust God.

This trust relationship begins for us in baptism. In baptism we are claimed as God's own. Following baptism, however, we encounter situations which make us afraid. Each of us has been, is, or will be afraid of something. Fear increases our pain. In most instances, when we are afraid of something, it hurts more if what we are afraid of happens. In our fear, God wrestles with us to bring us to trust in God. Regardless of what happens, God is saying, "Trust me."

God certainly wrestles with us in prayer when we are afraid. In this context, I have two suggestions:

1. Admit your fear to God.

2. Take time in prayer to listen to what God is saying. God will wrestle with us to bring us to a point of trust. Like Jacob, God will bring us to the place where God rules in our lives. In the midst of fear, this is the hope we have.

Written May 15, 2002

Praise, Sovereignty, and the Poor and Needy

"From the rising of the sun to its setting the name of the Lord is to be praised! The Lord is high above the nations, and his glory above the heavens! Who is like the Lord our God, who is seated on high, who looks far down upon the heavens and the earth? He raises the poor from the dust, and lifts the needy from the ash heap."

Psalm 113:3-7

The verses quoted above indicate three components of our faith. The first is praise of God. Praise is essential in that it directs attention away from us and towards God. Sometimes when facing stressful times, praise becomes difficult. At those times, we naturally turn inward upon ourselves. Author Philip Yancey speaks to this point. In his book, Where is God When It Hurts, he observes that when people focus on "Why did this tragedy happen to me?" they tend to be drawn away from God. Conversely, when people focus on "Where do we go from here?" they tend to be drawn closer to God. The "why" questions often defy answers. The response to tragedy of "Where do I go from here" leads to greater faith. It is forward looking. Let's be forward looking and praise God.

The second component is the sovereignty of God. God is Lord over all things. Many things that happen are not caused by God, nor are they God's will, but God is supreme over them. To put it another way, God is stronger than the events themselves. For example, the tragedy of September 11th was not caused by God nor was it God's will, but God is Lord over it. Another example: God did not cause my ALS, and it isn't God's will; but God is Lord over the ALS. In other words, God is stronger than ALS. Knowing that God is Lord over all things gives us the freedom and optimism to worship and serve.

Third, God is on the side of the poor and needy. This is helpful in two ways. First, when we are down and out God works to uplift us. This may come through worship. It may come through reading scripture. It may come through the actions of others. It may come through what you do. It may come over time. The point is: It is God's will to uplift us. Second, if God is on the side of the poor and needy, we should be on their side, too. We are God's hands to uplift those in need. This is God's call to each of us.

Written June 15, 2002

Look to the Future

"And I saw the holy city, new Jerusalem, coming down out of heaven from God, prepared as a bride adorned for her husband; and I heard a loud voice from the throne saying, 'Behold, the dwelling of God is with mortals. He will dwell with them, and they shall be his people, and God himself will be with them; he will wipe away every tear from their eyes, and death shall be no more, neither shall there be mourning nor crying nor pain any more, for the former things have passed away.'"

Revelation 21:2-4

Remember when you were a child how slowly time passed. A year seemed to take forever. As you grew older, time passed much more quickly. "Where has the time gone?" is a common expression. This life is passing rapidly. The good news is that God has provided a future for us. This future is envisioned in the text quoted above. The phrase "new Jerusalem" refers to the people of God – the church, of which you are a part. As the church, we will be presented to God as the apple of God's eye. Secondly, those things which cause pain now will be eliminated. Things like illness, tension, grief, war, and poverty will be former things. We do well to contemplate the future.

In his book, *The Problem of Pain*, C.S. Lewis makes the point that the reason Christians seem powerless in this life is that they don't think about the next life. The reverse of this is also true: Thinking about the future, which God has provided, will empower us today. When problems of any sort overwhelm you, looking to the future will keep you going. When you weary of well doing, a focus on the future will enable you to persist. When prayers seem not to be answered, a look to the future will keep you praying. Let's look to the future, which God has planned. It directs how we live today.

Written July 15, 2002

Trust God

"Humble yourselves therefore under the mighty hand of God, that in due time he will exalt you. Cast all your anxieties on him, for he cares about you."

1 Peter 5:6-7

To "humble yourself...under the might hand of God" involves trusting God. It means trusting God when things are not going well. It means trusting God when we don't understand what God is doing, or when it seems like God is doing nothing. God doesn't cause bad things to happen; God obviously allows them to happen. Humbling yourself means trusting God when bad things happen. The good news is this: the bad things won't last.

The verse continues with "That in due time God may exalt you." God is promising to exalt us. That may come partially in this life; it most definitely will occur fully in the age to come. This means that in the face of evil God wins. Because God wins, we will eventually win too. I appreciate the line in a hymn that reads, "Though the wrong seems oft so strong God is the ruler yet." (Lutheran Book of Worship, pg. 554) Because God is the ruler yet, we can serve God. We can work to make the world what God wants it to be.

"Cast all your anxieties on him..." Once again the issue is trusting God. When I was a swimming instructor, the most difficult facet of the job was to convince people the water would hold them up. When that was accomplished, the battle was won. Occasionally, an unexpected wave would cause the students to doubt, but the water still held them up. In a more wonderful way, God holds us up. Occasionally, an unexpected wave of misfortune causes us to doubt, but God still holds us up. It's a matter of trusting God who cares for us.

Written August 1, 2002

The Essence of Faith

"For by grace you have been saved through faith; and this is not your own doing, it is the gift of God — not because of works, lest any man should boast. For we are his workmanship, created in Christ Jesus for good works, which God prepared beforehand, that we should walk in them."

Ephesians 2:8-10

These verses represent the essence of our faith and ethics. We are God's people forever by the goodness of God—God's grace. Frequently our sin plagues us with guilt. Our faith often vacillates. The good news is that God's grace in the death and resurrection of Jesus is stronger than our sin. It is stronger than our guilt. It is stronger than our weak faith. God's grace saves us. Ephesians 1:4 says it well, "Even as God chose us in Christ before the foundation of the world..." God chose you before time began. You are God's because God chose you in Christ. Thanks be to God.

Even our faith is God's doing. Faith is not a good work on our part. We don't achieve it by hard work. Faith, which binds us to God, is the work of God. Martin Luther says it this way, "I cannot by my own reason or understanding believe in Jesus or come to him, but the Holy Spirit calls me through the gospel..." When Christ is preached the Holy Spirit creates faith within us. Take every opportunity you can to hear Christ preached so the Holy Spirit can strengthen your faith.

"For we are God's workmanship created in Christ Jesus for good works..." This is unequivocal. We are the handiwork of God. We are meant to be good. We do good, not to become God's people, but because we are God's people. It is what God intends for us.

Written September 7, 2002

Intergenerational Sharing

"One generation shall laud thy works to another, and shall declare thy mighty acts."

Psalm 145:4

This verse contains a great truth. One generation indeed shares its faith with another. This is both comforting and challenging. It is comforting because we are already doing it. Parents and grandparents share faith with their children and grandchildren. Sunday School teachers share their faith with their students. Confirmation mentors share faith with confirmation students. I remember a time when I was emotionally down due to my illness. A pastor, a generation older than me, said, "We have a good Lord." Hearing him say that, knowing he had experienced things I had not, strengthened me and gave me renewed hope. It doesn't always go from older to younger. Often, it goes from younger to older. I can point to specific instances in which the straight forwardness and vibrancy of youth have encouraged and strengthened me.

It is challenging because we should do more of it. At Bethlehem, we are not an old congregation. We are not a young congregation. In terms of age, we are diverse. There are many generations represented at Bethlehem, and this is our strength. Let's be intentional about sharing our faith with other generations. Let's listen when others share their faith. In this way, we are united in Christ. That's how it is meant to be.

Written October 1, 2002

Dependence on God

"And he humbled you and let you hunger and fed you with manna, which you did not know, nor did your fathers know; that he might make you know that man does not live by bread alone, but that man lives by everything that proceeds out of the mouth of the Lord. Your clothing did not wear out upon you, and your foot did not swell, these forty years."

Deuteronomy 8:3-4

God's people had just completed a difficult forty-year experience in the wilderness. They were about to enter a new land. These lines from Deuteronomy were written to remind them of two essential facts:

1. Though they had experienced difficulty, God had sustained them.

2. As they entered the new land they were to remember their dependence on God. Those two principles apply to us today also.

Certainly we live with difficulty too. God does not cause these difficulties, but certainly allows them. Yet, God sustains us. Personally, I sometimes feel anger toward God for not healing me. I become impatient at the pace of medical research. Yet, God sustains me. God sustains and strengthens each of us.

It is imperative that we remember our dependence on God. When we are healthy, and life is going reasonably well, it is easy to lose this sense of dependence. How quickly things can change. I went from being physically active to living in a wheel chair. In the midst of these changes God doesn't change, nor does God's love for us. When good things are taken away due to life's unpredictability, God is still there. God is the source of our strength and, ultimately, of all good things. We depend on God. We owe God our worship, praise, and thanksgiving.

Written November 15, 2002

Jesus Isn't the Reason: He Is the Answer

"For to you is born this day in the city of David a Savior, who is Christ the Lord."

Luke 2:11

This is an awesome message. The birth of Jesus means many things. It means God has come to us. It means we do not need to make ourselves acceptable to God; God makes us acceptable through Jesus. It means every sin is forgiven. We need not live lives plagued with guilt. It means we have an everlasting future with God. It means we serve God and others, not to make ourselves acceptable to God, but because God has come to us. This is joyful good news.

Too often our Christmas activities don't yield this kind of joy. For many people, this is a lonely time. Often our family gatherings do not live up to expectations or are accompanied by tension. Frequently we are glad when Christmas is over. When Christmas is viewed in its historical context, these problems are not surprising. Jesus' birth wasn't celebrated until approximately 400 AD. At that time there were various festivals, centering on the shortest days of the year, protesting winter's darkness. Since these festivals were unfulfilling, the church began celebrating the birth of Jesus as the light of the world who had come to us. Seen in this context, Jesus is not so much "the reason for the season," as the answer to the season. This Christmas, and as we begin a new year, let's focus on Jesus—the light of the world come to us.

Written December 1, 2002

A Brighter Day

"But Joseph said to them, 'Fear not, for am I in the place of God? As for you, you meant evil against me; but God meant it for good, to bring it about that many people should be kept alive, as they are today. So do not fear; I will provide for you and your little ones.' Thus he reassured them and comforted them."

Genesis 50:19-21

These verses are the culmination of the Joseph story in the book of Genesis. Joseph was sold by his brothers as a slave. Later he was unjustly imprisoned. In time God created a brighter day for Joseph. He not only was released from prison, but also became the number two man in Egypt. From this position of authority, he saved the Egyptians and his family from starvation during a severe famine. Following the death of their father, Joseph's brothers feared he might take revenge on them. Joseph forgave them and said, "…you meant evil against me; but God meant it for good…"

There are two points from this story on which I want to focus. First, we never know when God might create a brighter day for us. Though God sustained Joseph in prison, and was in fact good to him there, Joseph longed for release. I suspect there were days when Joseph wondered if release would ever come. In time God acted in a mighty way. It's the same way with us. When difficult times come to us, though God sustains us, we too long for release. At times we feel God has forgotten us. Yet, we never know what God will do and when God will do it. God might act soon. As God's people, we have every reason to be hopeful as we wait for God to act. Second, is God's relationship with us. God has claimed Joseph and was not about to let go. Through slavery, imprisonment, and in good times Joseph was God's own. It is the same for us. God has claimed us and will not let go. What if that brighter day never comes in this life? What if, despite our best efforts, things don't change? In that case, our relationship with God trumps the evil which befalls us. We were created for this relationship with God. It is what makes us fully human. Thanks be to God who claimed us. Thanks be to God who will not let go.

Written January 5, 2003

God's Call

Read Isaiah 6:1-8

These verses are God's call to Isaiah to be a prophet. This call from God exemplifies two aspects of our worship service. One is confession and forgiveness. The other is when we conclude with our mission statement.

When confronted with the presence of God, Isaiah exclaims in verse 5, "Woe is me! For I am lost; for I am a man of unclean lips, and I dwell in the midst of a people of unclean lips; for my eyes have seen the King, the Lord of hosts!" This is Isaiah's confession. Upon hearing this confession, God graciously offers forgiveness. Like Isaiah, sin is a very real part of our lives too. Sin separates us from God and divides us from others. Most Sundays we open our worship by confessing the sin in our lives. God graciously offers forgiveness to us. This forgiveness is boldly declared.

We are then free to live as God's forgiven people. This was true for Isaiah. This is true for us. In verse 8, God asks Isaiah, "Whom shall I send, and who will go for us?" Isaiah responds, "Here am I! Send me." This is akin to when we say, "We go now to share the good news of God's love." We are sent to live our daily lives as God's people. The challenge to each of us is to discover those ways, individually and collectively, to share the good news of God's love. This is God's call to each of us.

Written February 2, 2003

Doubt

"I believe; help my unbelief!"

Mark 9:2-4

This verse expresses both belief and doubt. Its source is a story in which Jesus heals an epileptic boy. Jesus said, "All things are possible to the one who believes." The boy's father then said, "I believe; help my unbelief."

We have times of doubt also. When prayers aren't answered as desired, when God doesn't act in desired ways, or when God doesn't seem to act at all, doubt arises. This is normal. It is imperative to note that, in the story, Jesus does not condemn the man's doubt. He does not condemn our doubt either. Furthermore, doubt is not overcome by "trying harder." To think "if only I believed more fully" or "if only I had more faith" is futile. This does not overcome doubt. When Jesus said, "All things are possible to the one who believes," he is asking us to look to him. Doubt is overcome by looking to Christ.

I will submit that doubt is one facet of faith and, ironically, works to strengthen it. In other words, faith includes doubt. For example, if all prayers were answered as desired and if God always acted in desired ways, then our relationship with God would be based on a quid pro quo – not faith. Conversely, by experiencing doubt, we are thrown back on faith. Faith binds us to God during difficult times. Faith binds us to God when our circumstances do not make sense. Faith binds us to God irrevocably.

Written March 7, 2003

Chosen by God

"Blessed be the God and Father of our Lord Jesus Christ, who has blessed us in Christ with every spiritual blessing in the heavenly places, even as he chose us in him before the foundation of the world, that we should be holy and blameless before him."

Ephesians 1:3-4

These verses are an awesome message for us. Before time began you were chosen to belong to God—forever. You were chosen to belong to God before the world was created. Such is the work of God! Such is God's grace! Unfortunately we have trouble appreciating grace. Sometimes it is because of guilt. Furthermore, we live in a world that runs by the principle "If something is too good to be true, it probably is." In addition, we are used to having to earn our way. Thankfully God operates on a level far different from the world in which we live. God operates on grace. The fact is you were chosen to belong to God before time began. Thanks be to God.

Because you were chosen by God, you are blameless before God. Again, this is pure grace. Often, because of sin and guilt, we don't feel blameless. To this I have two suggestions. First, look to Christ. Look into his face. When we do this we see that his death and resurrection forgives every sin. We see that God operates on grace. We see the things we need to change in our lives. Second, if guilt comes from wrong done to others, make amends if possible. Here I paraphrase one of the twelve steps of AA which is to make amends to others except when doing so would cause more harm. While God forgives every sin, including those done to others, we often don't appreciate that forgiveness unless we make amends. If making amends is impossible, or would cause more harm, trust in God's forgiveness. The reality is this: because of Christ you are blameless before God.

Written April 4, 2003

Exile Experiences

"But they who wait for the Lord shall renew their strength, they shall mount up with wings like eagles, they shall run and not be weary, they shall walk and not faint."

Isaiah 40:31

This verse proclaims why we are people of hope. For a generation God's people had been exiled in a foreign country. Isaiah 40, in its entirety, is God's promise to deliver them. After spending a whole generation in captivity, the people experienced doubt about God's promise. This verse tells the people to wait expectantly for God to act.

We have our own "exile experiences." It might be an illness experienced personally or by a family member. It might be a time of great stress. It might be a seemingly unsolvable problem. It might be a time of grief. Whatever our "exile experience," God has promised to act. God might bring healing, physically, mentally, or emotionally, perhaps over a period of time. God might give added strength to endure a difficult situation, or peace within that situation. God might give new insight by which you can solve a problem. Always, when we breathe our last, God will act in a marvelous and mighty way. This verse tells us to wait expectantly for God to act. God has promised to do so.

Written May 9, 2003

Interdependent People

"Now you are the body of Christ and individually members of it."

1 Corinthians 12:27

This verse declares that we have a corporate identity. Our identity is corporate as well as individual. Previously, in 1st Corinthians 12, the apostle Paul likens the church to a human body where each organ is interdependent. We, as God's people, are thus interdependent. Paul carries the analogy further by declaring we are the body of Christ. We are Christ's presence in the world today. As such, we are interdependent and derive our identity from on another. Thank God this is so.

This means we don't need to face life alone. We have, and need, each other. This is important for a number of reasons. The first reason is worship. God's word is preached when we are together. The sacraments are administered when we are together. Therefore, together we grow in our faith. The second reason is that we don't have to go it alone in life. The problems are too many; the temptations are too frequent; tragedies occur too often to go it alone. We are strong when we are together. We need the support of each other. We need to be accountable to each other. An illustration might be helpful. One stick is easily broken. Conversely, a fistful of sticks are hard to break. We are like those sticks: together we are strong. Third, we depend on the prayers of others. Fourth, each of us has unique talents and perspectives. No one can do everything. Everyone can do something. When we use our unique talents and perspectives for the common good, we are all strengthened and the church's outreach is enhanced. Thank God for each other.

Written June 5, 2003

Life's Unfairness

"For the word of the cross is folly to those who are perishing, but to us who are being saved it is the power of God."

1 Corinthians 1:18

The cross, with its suffering and death, is God's power to change the world. There were those who demanded powerful signs from God. To them the cross, with its suffering and death, made no sense. It seemed like folly. There were those who desired to approach God via human wisdom. The cross made no sense to them either. The cross, however, is where God chose to act. The cross is God's power to forgive, save, and redirect humankind.

Often our lives are plagued with guilt. Sometimes the guilt is so severe that the gospel message of forgiveness and salvation seems too good to be true. These doubts are based on human wisdom. In chapter 2 of 1st Corinthians, the writer declares that he doesn't preach in human wisdom lest one's faith be based on human wisdom and not the power of God. The cross is God's power to forgive and save you. Look to the cross and witness God's power.

This is important for another reason. It is no secret that life is unfair. The cross was unfair, too. Consequently, Jesus experienced life's unfairness. Therefore, during life's unfairness, God's power is present. It might be the power to change our circumstances. Even if our circumstances don't change, it is the power to bring hope for a better day. It is the power to bring hope to others. In life's unfairness is the power to bring change and hope.

Written July 4, 2003

Wonderful Works of God

"But you are a chosen race, a royal priesthood, a holy nation, God's own people, that you may declare the wonderful deeds of him who called you out of darkness into his marvelous light."

1 Peter 2:9

This is good news. You are God's because God chose you. It is the same for all of us. We are God's by God's choice. God man a choice for us. It is all by God's choice. It has nothing to do with us. If our relationship with God was based on our good works, we would never be sure we had done enough. If our relationship with God was based on our commitment, how can we be sure we are committed enough? Even our faith wavers. Thank God our relationship with God doesn't depend on the uncertainties of our lives. Because God has made a decision for us, what should we do? Serve and repent. Repentance means turning oneself around. It means making changes. What changes are needed in your life? What changes are needed in my life? Because God has chosen us, we are constantly making changes.

This verse gives us a job description. It is to "declare the wonderful works of God..." Our job description is to declare the wonderful works of God so that others will realize they are chosen also. To this I have three suggestions. One, invite people to worship. Most people will appreciate being invited. Two, do everything we do in such a way that it honors God. Three, a challenge to each of us is to find those ways in which we can naturally talk about our faith. We do these things because God has chosen us.

Written August 13, 2003

Emptying Oneself

"Have no anxiety about anything, but in everything by prayer and supplication with thanksgiving let your requests be made known to God."

Philippians 4:6

"Have no anxiety about anything..." That is a tall order. Each age has had anxiety producing aspects. This obviously includes our own age. We are invited, even commanded, to bring the causes of our anxiety to God. Often, God will change and redirect us so that we can deal with the cause, or causes, of our anxiety. An important ingredient to prayer is thankfulness. Thankfulness changes our perspective. It changes us from a "poor me" attitude to a realization of what God has done.

What happens when prayers aren't answered as desired, or seem not to be answered at all? The answer, it seems to me, is emptying oneself. This means emptying oneself of what we want so that we can appreciate what God does or doesn't do. Emptying oneself is the only way God's peace is realized in our lives. Perhaps a personal example would be helpful. At a recent ALS support group meeting the question was asked, "Are you accepting ALS as part of your lifestyle, or are you fighting it?" I must confess that I have been fighting it. Emptying myself of the desire to fight the disease is the only way to realize God's peace. I must add that emptying yourself doesn't constitute giving up. Certainly I want a cure. Certainly I want God's healing. Emptying myself of the desire to fight the disease is the only way to an awareness of God's peace. The key is emptying yourself to appreciate what God does or doesn't do. When we empty ourselves, the succeeding verse comes to pass which is, "And the peace of God, which passes all understanding, will keep your hearts and your minds in Christ Jesus."

Written September 10, 2003

A Place for You

"In my Father's house are many rooms; if it were not so, would I have told you that I go to prepare a place for you? And when I go and prepare a place for you, I will come again and will take you to myself, that where I am you may be also."

John 14:2-3

The first Sunday in November is All Saints Sunday. It is a day to give thank for those who have gone before us and to rejoice in the future God had prepared for us also. Shortly after I became a pastor, an elderly person asked me if it was wrong to pray that she might die. I don't remember what I said, but no, it isn't wrong. After experiencing suffering and pain, it is not wrong to desire relief. For others, death is a hard thing. It means separation from those we love and a severing of cherished relationships. Sometimes death comes tragically. Whatever our experiences, the good news is that God has prepared a future for us. In this future, there will be no separation. In fact, we will be reunited with those we love. In this future, there will be no pain and suffering. Those things will be banished. In this future, there will be no sin or guilt. Those will be former things.

In response to this good news, what should we do? I have three suggestions:

1. Be hopeful. In the Bible, hope is always expressed as a certainty. We have certainty of a future with God.

2. Be thankful. Be thankful for those we love who have gone before us. Thankfulness is a way of easing our grief. Thankfulness doesn't come initially; but it does come.

3. Let's work together. As victors through Christ, let's work to alleviate suffering in this world.

Written October 12, 2003

Theological Struggles

What do you do when prayers aren't answered as desired, or seem not to be answered at all? This has been a personal struggle for me. I would suspect for you, also. I have prayed for healing and for a cure, neither of which has happened. Perhaps you have also prayed for things which haven't occurred. I confess to occasional anger toward God because of this. As I wrote in a devotion a couple months ago, the answer is emptying oneself. By this I mean emptying ourselves of what we want so that we are ready for what God does or doesn't do. This is a tall order, especially when our wants are legitimate and appropriate. Perhaps only Jesus emptied himself perfectly. Never the less, it seems to me, this is the only way to prevent anger towards God when God doesn't do what we want. Personally, what this means is, that though I crave God's healing or a cure, I need to empty myself to the extent that if neither happens I can accept it.

Closely akin to this is the concept of doubt. When bad things happen, sometimes doubt arises. I will submit that doubt is not the opposite of faith but is actually a component of faith. When doubt arises, it drives us to God simply because there is no one else to whom we can go. In this way, doubt strengthens faith. What this means regarding my illness is that sometimes I doubt God's love. To have the power to heal and not use it doesn't seem very loving. It isn't only me. You all know people who have prayed for healing and not received it. What my doubt does is drive me to God because there is no one else to whom to go. In this way, doubt strengthens my faith.

The other thing I want to say is never underestimate yourselves. I have gained a renewed appreciation of Paul's theology of the church as the Body of Christ. This means that God speaks and acts through you. In this respect, you are the presence of Christ in the world today. Many times during this illness I have wondered where God is, only to hear God speaking and see God acting through you. It seems that God has left the solution to many problems with the Body of Christ.

Problems such as hunger and injustice are left to us to solve. Never underestimate yourselves; you are the Body of Christ.

Written November 23, 2003

Born Again, and Again

"Do you not know that all of us who have been baptized into Christ Jesus were baptized into his death? We were buried therefore with him by baptism into death, so that as Christ was raised from the dead by the glory of the Father, we too might walk in newness of life."

Romans 6:3-4

A new year is a time for a fresh start—right? New Year's resolutions, despite our best intentions, are often broken. Human will power is insufficient. We need something more. We need to return to our baptism. Some basic theology of baptism is helpful in this context. In the water of our baptism God drowns our sinful self and we rise as God's people. This is a new birth. You can say that in baptism we are born again. However, our sinful self keeps raising its ugly head. Therefore, we need to return to our baptism each day. This means we die to ourselves each day and rise to live as God's people. In answer to the question "Are you born again?" the appropriate answer is yes—again and again and again.

This has practical application for daily life and for a new year. When we are tempted, either to do something we know is wrong or not do something we know is right, human will power is often not enough. We need to return to our baptism. This means we die to our desires and rise to live as God's people. The second application is confession. When we know we have sinned, we lean on the mercy of God in confession. In essence, we die to ourselves and rise to live as God's forgiven people. The third application is personal problems. On a particular day, not too long ago, I was feeling not a little sorry for myself. The temptation was to dump on people around me. I had to die to my self-centeredness and rise to say more constructive things to those around me. At other times, this means to die to the way things are and rise to follow God's leading and make positive changes in our lives. In Christ we die in order to fully live.

Written December 6, 2003

Grace

"For our sake he made him to be sin who knew no sin, so that in him we might become the righteousness of God. Working together with him, then, we entreat you not to accept the grace of God in vain. For he says, 'At the acceptable time I have listened to you, and helped you on the day of salvation.' Behold, now is the acceptable time; behold, now is the day of salvation."

2 Corinthians 5:21-6:2

"…God made him (Jesus) to be sin who knew no sin…" Jesus, at the cross, experienced our sin. Though he had no sin, he experienced ours. This is pure grace. This means every sin is forgiven. This means those sins which cause us the deepest anguish and guilt are forgiven. God doesn't hold them against us. This means we don't need to confess the same sin over and over again. Once is enough. Sometimes, in our guilt, this seems too good to be true. The good news is that our faith is based, not on how we feel, but on Jesus Christ. Jesus went to the cross for our sins and rose to life again. Through Jesus, God forgives every one of our sins.

What do we do with this grace? We repent. Repentance means nothing less than turning our lives around. Because of God's grace in Jesus we turn our lives around. This is the meaning of "…we entreat you not to accept the grace of God in vain." Lest we accept the grace of God in vain we repent—we turn our lives around. What are we doing that we shouldn't, or what are we not doing that we should? These are the kind of changes God asks us to make. These changes constitute repentance. Because God forgives us we repent—we turn our lives around.

Written January 10, 2004

Pray, Trust, Praise

"How long, O Lord? Wilt thou forget me forever? How long wilt thou hide they face from me?"

Psalms 13:1

The Psalm writer felt abandoned by God. We don't know what the specific circumstance was, but the sense of abandonment was definitely present. On two other occasions in the Psalm the writer uses the phrase "How long." Most of us have had, or will have, times when we feel abandoned by God also.

God, through the Psalm writer, gives us three tools to use when we feel this sense of abandonment. Verse three reads, "Consider and answer me, O Lord my God..." This verse alludes to prayer. When feeling abandoned by God—pray. Often, when we feel abandoned by God, prayers don't seem to be answered. When this happens, look back. When we do this, we see that God has carried us. If God has carried us in the past, this indicates God will carry us in the future. Otherwise, God may strengthen us for the situation or give us a new perspective on it. God may remove the situation or may give us a new way of dealing with it. Verse five reads, "But I have trusted in thy steadfast love..." When feeling abandoned by God—trust God. This may seem ironic, but it is true. What is the object of our trust? It is God's love. The cross is the ultimate sign of God's love. God, who went to the cross for us, certainly wants what is best for us. In an imperfect world, tragedies happen. Be assured that these tragedies are not God's will. In fact, the cross is God's embrace of us in the midst of tragedy. Verse six reads, "I will sing to the Lord, because he has dealt bountifully with me." This connotes praise. When feeling abandoned by God—praise God. Praise focuses our attention on what God has done. When our attention is on what God has done, we feel less abandoned. Besides, what God has done portends what God will do. Prayer, trust, praise—these are tools which God has given us. Let's use them.

Written February 6, 2004

A Tent vs. A House

"For we know that if the earthly tent we live in is destroyed, we have a building from God, a house not made with hands, eternal in the heavens."

II Corinthians 5:1

Have you ever slept in a tent? Usually when we do that there is a tree root or a rock in the wrong place, making sleep difficult. Sleeping in a tent is fun, but it is not the real thing. Paul, in the verse quoted above, describes life as we know it as living in a tent. Life as we know it can be fun, but it is not the real thing. Conversely, Paul describes the resurrection to come as living in a house—not a tent. In other words, the age to come is better. The contrast between a tent and a house is one way of illustrating the difference between life as we know it and the age to come. The age to come is God's promise to us.

The next verse reads, "Here indeed we groan, and long to put on our heavenly dwelling." There is much groaning in this "tent." Some groan under illness or handicap. Some groan under poverty and hunger. Some groan under injustice and oppression. Some groan with grief. Some groan because life is missing something. In the resurrection to come, God will take us out of this tent and give us a house. In other words, in the resurrection to come, all groaning will cease. It even gets better. We have a relationship with God that now strengthens us in the midst of our groaning.

Conversely, for some life is good. There is minimal, if any, groaning. If you are one of these people, thank God it is so. One thing this illness has taught me is that life is uncertain. The end can come at any time. When the end does come, in spite of how good life has been, it will get infinitely better. God will take us out of this tent and give us a house in which to live. Thank God this is so.

Written March 5, 2004

Places of God's Presence

"If I take the wings of the morning and dwell in the uttermost parts of the sea, even there thy hand shall lead me, and thy right hand shall hold me."

Psalms 139:9 & 10

God is with us—period. Nothing can happen to us where God is not present. We can go nowhere, where God is not with us. This does not mean that everything that happens to us is God's will. Frequently, things happen to us that are not the will of God. Why these things happen, I do not know. When these things happen, God may work them out for our good in this life. God will always give us a future beyond our wildest dreams. Such is our baptismal calling. God may not have every word, but God definitely has the last word. This is the God who is with us always.

How is God with us? First, God comes to us in the spoken word. When Christ is preached, the Holy Spirit creates faith within us. This faith, in turn, sustains us and makes us aware of God's presence. Second, God comes to us in the sacraments. In both baptism and communion, God comes to us. God sustains us in this way. Such is the importance of worship for comprehending God's presence. Third, I believe God comes to us and is with us in the presence of true friends. Friends may confront us, advise us, console us, or just be with us. As a take off on "What a Friend We Have in Jesus," I like Martin Marty's statement, "What a Jesus we have in a friend." Jesus comes in the presence of friends.

Because God is with us, we ought to honor God in all we do. In the context of the verse quoted above, the writer is justifying himself before God by saying, in essence, "Because you have always been with me, you know I haven't done anything wrong." While, because of Jesus, we no longer need to justify ourselves before God, the principle remains the same—we ought to honor God in all we do.

Written April 3, 2004

In Christ, We Are Strong

"My Grace is sufficient for you, for my power is made perfect in weakness..."

2 Corinthians 12:9

God's grace is sufficient for us; God will work through our weakness. That is the message of this verse. Paul, who wrote these lines, spoke in the preceding verses of a "thorn in the flesh." What this "thorn in the flesh" was we do not know. It may have been a physical illness or handicap. It may have been something else. It definitely was something that was beyond his control. Paul prayed that God would remove this "thorn in the flesh." God's answer was "no." Through prayer Paul came to realize that "God's grace was sufficient for him and that God's power is made perfect in weakness." God worked in a powerful way through Paul in spite of, and perhaps because of, his weakness. When he was weak, then he was strong.

Frequently, God does not remove problems from us that are beyond our control either, though we wish God would do so. Why God acts in this way, I do not know. Perhaps it is because if we realize our weakness we then lean on the One who is strong. In this way, we are stronger than we ever would be on our own. What I do know is this: God sustains us in our weakness and vulnerability and works through our weakness in spite of, and perhaps because of, that very weakness. When we are weak, then, in Christ we are strong.

Written May 1, 2004

The Treasure of Christ

"But we have this treasure in earthen vessels, to show that the transcendent power belongs to God and not to us. We are afflicted in every way, but not crushed; perplexed, but not driven to despair; persecuted, but not forsaken; struck down, but not destroyed;"

2 Corinthians 4:7-9

We constantly live with human limitations. Some limitations are physical. We are subject to disease and ultimately death. It is frustrating not to be able to do what we want to do or not be able to do what we used to do. Some limitations are moral. Often, we know what is right but have a difficult time doing it. When we encounter difficult times, perhaps the greatest limitation is our belief that God is not doing anything. Our tendency is to give up on God at these times. Such are the limits with which we live.

As we live with human limitations, we have the treasure of Christ. While Paul calls these limitations "earthen vessels", he makes certain we know that we possess the treasure of Christ at the same time. At the same time as we live with frustrating limits, we have hope through Christ. That is why he can write, "We are afflicted in every way, but not crushed; perplexed, but not driven to despair; persecuted, but not forsaken; struck down, but not destroyed;" Why is this so? It is because of Christ. Christ encountered the ultimate human limitation— death—and overcame it. Because of Christ, we can know that God is always at work. This is true even in the most trying of circumstances. Because of Christ, there is always hope for us.

Written June 8, 2004

Individualism vs. Christian Identity

"Yes, and I shall rejoice. For I know that through your prayers and help of the Spirit of Jesus Christ this will turn out for my deliverance, as it is my eager expectation and hope that I shall not be at all ashamed, but that with full courage now as always Christ will be honored in my body, whether by life or by death. For to me to live is Christ, and to die is gain."

Philippians 1:19-21

Paul, the author of these lines, was in jail at the time of their writing. He expressed confidence in the prayers of the people. In this we have a blueprint for our life together in Christ. We ought to pray for one another. Is someone hurting? Pray for that person. Is someone going through a difficult time? Pray for that person. Unfortunately, today the cultural emphasis is on individualism, particularly in matters of religion. Religion is thought to be a private matter. This negatively impacts our prayer and support for one another. Our Lord would not have it this way. Let's pray for one another.

Paul further writes, "To live is Christ..." He declares that his goal is to honor Christ in all he does. Such is our baptismal calling too. We are to honor Christ in all we do. In today's individualism, the tendency is to believe we are our own persons. We then feel we can do whatever we want. However, in baptism we are claimed by Christ. We are literally owned by Christ. Our destiny is to honor Christ in all that we do.

He further writes, "...and to die is gain." When we die, we will gain that which we have only partially at present. Perhaps an illustration will help. As we grow older, time passes more rapidly. In late June I heard many people say, "Where is the summer going?" I felt this way also. I am writing these lines in early July. By the time you read them, the summer will be two-thirds gone. Time flies. How good would it be if we had one good day after another, without time passing? Such is the future God has provided for us. In Christ, to die is indeed gain.

Written July 6, 2004

Our Source of Help

"I lift up my eyes to the hills. From whence does my help come? My help comes from the Lord, who made heaven and earth."

Psalm 121:1-2

The Psalm writer begins with a rhetorical question, "From where does my help come?" Does it come from the hills, thought to be the dwelling of the local gods, or does it come from the Lord? The writer answers emphatically, "My help comes from the Lord who made heaven and earth." Help did not come from the local deities but from the Lord. This begs the question for us—where do we look for our help? Implicit in the Psalm is that anything other than the Lord will, in the long run, produce disappointment. The Lord is our help, too.

When the writer says, "My help comes from the Lord who made heaven and earth," an important dynamic of our faith is stated. The Lord is God because the Lord creates. If some other entity created, that entity would, in fact, be God. The writer affirms, and we affirm every Sunday, that the Lord created heaven and earth. The Lord is God because the Lord creates. While the method of creation is best left to the domain of science, the Lord is the creator of heaven and earth. It is important to realize that creation is not a one time event. In fact, creation is on going. We could not take our next breath if it were not for the creative and life sustaining power of the Lord. Realizing that creation is on going, there is no limit to the help the Lord can give.

Another vital dynamic of our faith is stated. When we read this Psalm, the Holy Spirit creates faith within us. The Lord doesn't do everything we want. The Lord doesn't always do what we think is essential. However, when we read this Psalm, faith is created within us. With faith in the Lord, as revealed in Jesus Christ, we have all the help we need.

Written August 11, 2004

We Need Each Other

"I thank my God in all my remembrance of you, always in every prayer of mine for you all making my prayer with joy, thankful for your partnership in the Gospel from the first day until now."

Philippians 1:3-5

Paul begins by thanking God for the Philippian Christians. He indicated that he prays for them. He speaks of a partnership with them in the Gospel. In essence, they needed him and he needed them. They needed each other.

We need each other too. There are probably many reasons for this. I would like to talk about three of them. As I wrote on another occasion, many times during this illness I have wondered where God is at, only to hear God speaking and see God acting through you people. Often you have been the presence of Christ to me. However, it isn't only my situation. Most of us have had, or will have, times when God seems distant. At those times we are the presence of Christ to each other. The second reason is akin to the first: Christ comes to us in a special way through others. When we pray for others, when we listen to others, when we help others, Christ comes in a special way to them. Conversely, when others do these things for us, Christ comes to us in a special way. Let me give another example. Often, due to my illness, I am unable to attend worship. While I am thankful for the radio broadcast on those Sundays, it isn't the same as being in church and worshiping with people. We need to worship with others. Christ comes to us in a special way when we do so. The third reason is accountability. Paul writes of a partnership in the Gospel with the Philippian Christians. In any partnership, one partner is accountable to the others and the others are accountable to the one. We, at Bethlehem, are in partnership in the Gospel too. As such, we are accountable to each other. Through this accountability we are strengthened in our faith. For these reasons we need each other.

Written September 12, 2004

Evangelism and Social Ministry

"The Spirit of the Lord God is upon me, because the Lord has anointed me to bring good tidings to the afflicted, he has sent me to bind up the brokenhearted, to proclaim liberty to the captives, and the opening of the prison to those who are bound;"

Isaiah 61:1

In Luke, Jesus begins his public ministry by reading this verse from Isaiah. These words provide an overview of what Jesus was going to do. As people, baptized into Christ, this is our calling too. We are called to do the same things that Jesus did. This has awesome implications for evangelism and social ministry. In terms of evangelism, we are called to tell the good news of Jesus Christ. Some people are afflicted with the fear of dying. Many are captive to guilt. We live in a world of brokenhearted people. Our calling is to tell of the crucified and risen Christ. In Christ, everlasting life replaces the fear of dying. In Christ, forgiveness replaces guilt. Jesus has a word of hope for the brokenhearted. Most people enjoy being bearers of good news. This is precisely what we are called to do: to be bearers of the good news of Jesus Christ. In terms of social ministry, the challenge is before us. Many people are captive to hunger, injustice, and abuse. It does seem that God has left these problems for us to solve. Let's fulfill our calling to help these people. In terms of evangelism and social ministry, let's press onward.

Written October 2, 2004

A Repeat

"For to you is born this day in the city of David a Savior, who is Christ the Lord."

Luke 2: 11

This is an awesome message. The birth of Jesus means many things. It means God has come to us. It means we do not need to make ourselves acceptable to God; God makes us acceptable through Jesus. It means every sin is forgiven. We need not live lives plagued with guilt. It means we have an everlasting future with God. It means we serve God and others, not to make ourselves acceptable to God, but because God has come to us. This is joyful good news.

Too often our Christmas activities don't yield this kind of joy. For many people, this is a lonely time. Often our family gatherings do not live up to expectations or are accompanied by tension. Frequently we are glad when Christmas is over. Perhaps it is helpful to view Christmas in its historical setting. Jesus' birth wasn't celebrated until approximately 400 AD. At that time there were various festivals, centering on the shortest days of the year, protesting winter's darkness. Since these festivals were unfulfilling, the church began celebrating the birth of Jesus as the light of the world who had come to us. Seen in this context, Jesus is not so much "the reason for the season," as the answer to the season. This Christmas let's focus on Jesus—the answer to the season. Here are three suggestions for doing this. Worship more often. Read your bible more frequently. Do something that isn't required of you for someone else. I pray this will be a Christ-filled Christmas for each of you.

Written November 8, 2004

Praise God

"*From the rising of the sun to its setting the name of the Lord is to be praised!*"

Psalms 113:3

Praising God is the most significant spiritual endeavor in which we can engage. Praising God deepens and strengthens our faith. Often we don't feel like praising God. There are many reasons for this. It might be stress in our lives. It might be a tragedy that we have encountered. It might be that we have grown indifferent to the things God does for us. On some days, due to my illness, God seems light years away. On those days, I don't feel like praising God. However, this is a feeling; and feelings often deceive us. On a deeper level, one thing I have learned from this illness is that God is always with us—step by step. This is the reality with which we live. I could not make it through this illness were this not so. Whatever you are going through, God is with you. For this reason, we praise God. Let's praise God and grow in our faith.

Written December 10, 2004

Prayer — Communication with God

"*Likewise the Spirit helps us in our weakness; for we do not know how to pray as we ought, but that very spirit intercedes with sighs too deep for words. And God, who searches the heart, knows what is the mind of the Spirit, because the Spirit intercedes for the saints according to the will of God.*"

Romans 8:26-27

Prayer is communication with God. Sometimes we pray for ourselves and our needs. Sometimes we pray for others and their needs. Sometimes we thank God for what God has done and is doing. As with any communication we also listen. It is imperative that we listen to what God is saying to us. Occasionally God speaks immediately. Sometimes God speaks to us over a period of time, but God always speaks. We can count on that if we listen. Ironically, God sometimes speaks through silence.

What happens if we don't have the right words to say? What happens if we don't feel like praying? What happens if we are too exhausted to pray? What happens if we are too discouraged to pray? This discouragement may come from our circumstances or it may come from viewing the pain in the world around us. What happens in each of these cases? The Holy Spirit prays for us. The Holy Spirit intercedes for us. This is why prayer is a source of hope. Through our personal agony and through the agony of the world around us, prayer leads to a new birth of hope. Whether we obtain the answer we desire or not, prayer is a source of hope. Let's communicate with God and grow in hope.

Written January 8, 2005

God's Will Prevails

"We know that all things work together for good for those who love God, who are called according to his purpose."

Romans 8:28

Through baptism, God calls us. Through baptism, we are claimed as God's own. Through baptism we are born to everlasting life. However, baptism doesn't preclude bad things from happening to us. Obviously, they occur. When scripture says, "We know that all things work together for good...", it doesn't mean that all things are good or that God causes all things. God does not cause bad things to happen. For example, God didn't cause my illness. God didn't cause the Tsunami that ravaged southern Asia two months ago. God didn't cause whatever tragedies have befallen you. God does not cause bad things to happen, though God may use bad things when they do happen to teach us something. Rather, this verse means God's will, will prevail. No tragedy will impede God's will from being accomplished. God's will may be accomplished in this life. If so, thank God. Most certainly it will be accomplished in the age to come. Let's praise God because God's will prevails.

Written February 1, 2005

Jesus Strengthens Us

"I can do all things through him who strengthens me."

Philippians 4:13

Thankfulness pervades Paul's writings. In the lines prior to the verse quoted above, Paul writes "I have learned to be content with whatever I have." He talks about times of having little and about times of plenty. He talks about facing hunger and times of being well-fed. Not that he was thankful for the hunger or times of having little, but on the deepest level an attitude of thankfulness under girded his life. Paul was a thankful person. Why was this so? It was because he could "....do all things through him who strengthens me." He could endure all things through Jesus Christ who strengthened him. First, Jesus is with us - always. No tragedy, problem, or event can drive Jesus from us. Jesus is with us always. Second, God through Jesus became fully human. This means Jesus knows our tragedies and problems. He knows what it is like to die. In fact, the cross is God's embrace of us. In tragedies, problems, and ultimately our death, God embraces us. Third, He Is Risen. Jesus is alive. This means He has overcome our tragedies and problems. He has overcome our death, giving everlasting life to us. In the long run, everlasting life is what counts. We, too, can do all things through Jesus who strengthens us.

Written March 1, 2005

Suffering to Hope

"Therefore, since we are justified by faith, we have peace with God through our Lord Jesus Christ, through whom we have obtained access to this grace in which we stand; and we boast in our hope of sharing the glory of God. And not only that, but we also boast in our sufferings, knowing that suffering produces endurance, and endurance produces character, and character produces hope, and hope does not disappoint us, because God's love has been poured into our hearts through the Holy Spirit that has been given to us."

Romans 5:1-5

Often we are troubled by guilt. We feel guilty over things we have done. We feel guilty over things we should have done but didn't do. I have experienced these same feelings. The good news is this: "Therefore, since we are justified by faith, we have peace with god through our Lord Jesus Christ…" We are justified before God, not by the good things we have done, but by faith in Jesus. It gets even better. Paul writes, "…we rejoice in our hope of sharing the glory of God." We will share the glory of God. When Paul uses the word "hope" in this context, it connotes certainty. We rejoice in our hope, the certainty, of sharing the glory of God.

Paul writes about suffering. The irony is this: though God does not cause suffering, God will use suffering to increase our hope. I have said many times that God doesn't cause suffering, but God will use it. God will use suffering to mold us into more hopeful people. In other words, God will use it to make us more certain of sharing the glory of God.

How do we obtain hope and faith? They are God's gifts through the Holy Spirit. We don't conjure up faith by ourselves. We don't conjure up hope that way either. They are God's gifts through the Holy Spirit. Never feel that your faith is inadequate. It is God's gift to you. Through the Holy Spirit, we are people of faith and hope.

Written April 2, 2005

Reasons for Thankfulness

Bless the Lord, O my Soul, and all that is within me, bless his holy name. Bless the Lord, O my Soul, and do not forget all his benefits.

Psalms 103:1-2

These verses exhort us to thankfulness. They remind us to be mindful of the good that God does. Thankfulness is imperative as we live our Christian lives. Often, we are not thankful. There are many reasons for this. It may be some event that has occurred to us or a family member, or it may be that we have prayed and prayed for something - only to encounter God's silence. Possibly it is because we have come to take good things for granted. I admit that, before I developed ALS, I took good health for granted. When we have difficulty being thankful, it helps to look at the larger picture. The larger picture is this: Jesus died and rose from the dead to give us eternal life. We will spend eternity with God and our Christian friends. This is the larger picture. Once we are thankful for it, we can also be thankful for the smaller things such as good health, friendships, a safe night's rest, and other such things. The smaller things, too, are God's gifts to us. Indeed, thankfulness is imperative as we live our Christian faith.

Written May 1, 2005

God's Silence

"He said, 'Go out and stand on the mountain before the Lord, for the Lord is about to pass by.' Now there was a great wind, so strong that it was splitting mountains and breaking rocks in pieces before the Lord, but the Lord was not in the wind; and after the wind an earthquake; and after the earthquake a fire, but the Lord was not in the fire; and after the fire a sound of sheer silence."

1 Kings 19:11-12

This is about Elijah, the Old Testament prophet. In Chapters 17 and 18 Elijah, with God's help, did some powerful things. God seemed very close to Elijah. Most of us have had experiences like that, when God seemed very close. Thank God for those times.

Most of us have also had experiences like Chapter 19, when God seemed far away. In Elijah's case, the queen was after his life. His work seemed like a failure. Everything seemed hopeless, and Elijah wanted to die. When he prayed, he encountered the "sound of sheer silence." Most of us have had experiences like that. We have prayed and prayed for something only to encounter God's silence. This is very frustrating. I have experienced that frustration. Why does God do this? I believe it is, ironically, to increase our trust in God. In the short term, this is very frustrating. In the long term, it increases our trust in God. Once God gained Elijah's trust, Elijah realized God had been there all along. In addition, in the later part of Chapter 19, God gave direction to Elijah. It is the same with us. Once God gains our trust, we realize God has been there all along. We become thankful for things we once took for granted. In addition, once God gains our trust, God gives direction to us. In the course of life, this process is repeated many times. God uses silence to increase our trust.

Written June 4, 2005

God's Possessions

"The earth is the Lord's and all that is in it, the world, and those who live in it."

Psalms 24:1

This verse makes clear that God possesses all things. The environment in which we live belongs to God. The things to which we have title really belong to God. God owns everything. As the verse makes clear, "The earth is the Lord's and all that is in it..." Our work and efforts to achieve give us temporary control over things, but ultimately God is the owner. Would we want it any other way? I don't think so. If we were the ultimate owners of things, that would make us gods. What a mess that would be. God is God precisely because God owns all things.

This has pivotal implications for living our Christian faith. The first implication is for stewardship. Because God possesses all things, it is imperative that we handle wisely the things over which we have temporary control. God needs those things over which we have temporary control to help those who control very little. God needs us to help those who have little. As the verse above makes clear, the poor belong to God also. The poor are our sisters and brothers. The other implication is our care for the environment in which we live. In our youth we learned to respect that which belonged to another. Since the environment belongs to God, let's respect and care for it. Let's respect and take care of what really belongs to God.

Written July 1, 2005

Worship and Education

"Go therefore and make disciples of all nations, baptizing them in the name of the Father and of the Son and of the Holy Spirit, and teaching them to obey everything that I have commanded you. And remember, I am with you always, to the end of the age."

Matthew 28:19-20

Jesus makes clear that the main function of the church, in other words all of us, is to make disciples for him. This involves both evangelism and education. In terms of evangelism, we are to reach out with the good news of Jesus to all people. However, at the beginning of our education year I would like to focus on that topic, as Jesus said, "...teaching them to obey everything I have commanded you..." In this context, worship and education go together. Both are necessary to grow as disciples of Jesus. Worship feeds the heart; education feeds the head. Both are necessary. With this in mind, I have two suggestions. Parents, bring your children to worship. They are already receiving education in Sunday School. Their heads are being fed; feed their hearts also. I realize this is sometimes difficult, but I encourage you to do it. Secondly, if you are able, attend adult Christian education. This will help you to obey the things Jesus commanded us to do. These things will help us to grow as disciples of Christ.

Written August 1, 2005

God Knows Us

"O Lord, you have searched me and known me. You know when I sit down and when I rise up; you discern my thoughts from far away. You search out my path and my lying down, and are acquainted with all my ways. Even before a word is on my tongue, O Lord, you know it completely. You hem me in, behind and before, and lay your hand upon me. Such knowledge is too wonderful for me; it is so high that I cannot attain it."

Psalm 139:1-6

God knows all about us. These verses make this fact very clear. God knows all about us—and forgives us. In fact, the cross is God's embrace of us in our sin and guilt. At the cross Jesus became so identified with us that our sin became his and his goodness became ours. Such is God's magnificent grace. What do we do with this grace and forgiveness? We thank God—and repent. Repentance means making 180 degree turns in our lives. It means turning away from those things which we know are sinful and living as God intends for us. We repent, not to achieve God's forgiveness, but because God has already forgiven us.

When we pray, we pray to this all-knowing God. Sometimes, however, our prayers seem unanswered. Why is this so? There are many reasons; I would like to talk about two of them. The first is that this world is out of sync with God. The world in which we live is essentially hostile to God. For this reason, God's will is sometimes unaccomplished in the short term. God's will is always accomplished in the long term. The second reason is directly related to the above text. God always desires what is best for us. Sometimes the things for which we ask are not always in our best interests. Suffice it to say that God knows what is best for us and is working to that end.

Written September 1, 2005

Where Can I Go From Your Presence?

"Where can I go from your spirit? Or where can I flee from your presence? If I ascend to heaven, you are there; if I make my bed in Sheol, you are there."

Psalms 139:7-8

God is with us—always. In fact, we can do nothing apart from God's presence. In the Old Testament, "Sheol" was considered a shadowy abode of the dead. The concept of resurrection to everlasting life was largely undeveloped at that time. The writer is saying that even if he makes his "bed in Sheol" (this shadowy abode of the dead), God is still present. Jesus makes it even better. On the first Sunday in November we celebrate All Saints Sunday. This is a celebration of our certainty of resurrection to everlasting life. Through Jesus we will "ascend to heaven." Even though we die, we are still in God's presence.

This presence of God has bearing on our hope today. Despair surrounds us. We experience illness. We hear of war and hurricanes (I am writing this in the aftermath of hurricanes Katrina and Rita.) One day when watching CNN, I had to ask someone to turn the TV off saying, "I can't take any more bad news." However, even in our despair, we are people with hope. Why? It is because the presence of God permeates our despair and gives us hope. In Christ, God is with us constantly. In Christ, we are people with hope.

Written October 7, 2005

The Word Became Flesh

"And the word became flesh and lived among us, and we have seen his glory, the glory as of a father's only son, full of grace and truth."

John 1:14

In the first five verses of John, chapter 1, several things are said about the Word of God. The Word existed before all things. The Word is the agent of creation. The Word is the source of our life and light. Then in verse 14, we read "and the Word became flesh and lived among us..." The Word of God came to us as Jesus. We are preparing to celebrate his coming and birth.

It is no secret that our Christmas celebrations are both secular and sacred. Our secular celebrations can be both fun and rewarding. They can also be draining. Sometimes, because of our secular celebrations, Christmas is a lonely, frustrating, and emotionally and physically draining time. Often we are glad when it is over. Contrast this with Jesus, the Word of God, coming to us. Jesus comes with friendship, love, hope, and grace. Jesus comes with direction for living and with a better way to live. During this month let's focus on Jesus, the Word of God, coming to us.

Written November 1, 2005

Patience

"I waited patiently for the Lord; he inclined to me and heard my cry."

Psalm 40:1

Patience is a difficult virtue to learn - at least for me. I always operated on the premise that if something needed to be done, it needed to be done now. This is particularly frustrating with ALS. While ALS causes no physical pain, it sorely tries my patience. What I have learned through this illness is that God simply does not operate on our time schedule. Sometimes God works faster than we desire and sometimes God works slower than we desire, but God doesn't work on our time schedule. It was Henri Nouwen who said, "Hope without patience is wishful thinking." God is a God of hope, but without patience we are likely to become angry and frustrated with God. Note the progression in the text written above. The writer first has patience and then realizes what God has done. This is how it works in our Christian faith. When we have patience, we realize what God is doing in our lives and in the world around us. Patience is worth learning.

Written December 2, 2005

Dynamics of the Church

"I have told the glad news of deliverance in the great congregation; see, I have not restrained my lips, as you know, O Lord."

Psalm 40:9

The Psalm writer knew the essence of being part of a community of faith. That was to share one's faith with other members of the same community of faith. God has also placed us in a community of faith—the church—for many reasons. One reason is that we might share our faith with other members of the church and so strengthen one another. We have been conditioned to think faith is a private matter and so find sharing our faith difficult. This is unfortunate because it inhibits what we can do for each other. I have four suggestions for sharing our faith. The first is simply to talk about Jesus. When we say the name of Jesus, the Holy Spirit works through that to edify us all. The second is to be more open in sharing our faith. When we don't know something, it is okay to say, "I don't know" or "I don't understand that." When we share our faith with each other, we all are strengthened. The third suggestion is to listen to each other. Just listen. Don't worry about what you will say in response. Just listen. I read somewhere that listening is the highest honor we can give someone. When we listen to someone, we are the presence of Christ to him or her. The fourth is to pray for one another. It is amazing what God will do in our midst when we bring each others needs before God. Let's share our faith with each other.

Written January 1, 2006

Amazing Grace

"Ho, everyone who thirsts, come to the waters; and you that have no money. Come, buy and eat! Come, buy wine and milk without money and without price."

Isaiah 55:1

This is a metaphor for God's grace. God's people were exiled in a foreign land, and God was about to bring them home. This was pure grace. This text is God's invitation to participate in that grace. Jesus invites us also to participate in that grace. We also are in a kind of exile. We are exiled from God because of our sin. Jesus offers forgiveness and reconciliation. This is pure grace. He invites us to participate in that grace. We are exiled from God due to death. On Ash Wednesday we will hear, "You are dust and to dust you shall return." Jesus will raise us up to everlasting life. This is pure grace. Jesus invites us to participate in this grace. Jesus offers us a new beginning in life. Once again, this is pure grace. These changes are wrought by God's grace and love. What about things that don't change, such as the daily grind of an illness? In that case, we are supported and surrounded by God's grace and love. This grace and love gives birth to hope. In hope, we know that sometime the unchangeable will change. Come, participate in God's grace.

Written February 1, 2006

Mighty Acts of God

"But you are a chosen race, a royal priesthood, a holy nation, God's own people, in order that you may proclaim the mighty acts of him who called you out of darkness into his marvelous light."

I Peter 2:9

Your faith is no accident. When God chose you, God put faith in your life. As the text says, "...you are a chosen race..." We didn't so much choose God, but God chose us. What about when our faith is sorely tried? What about when prayers seem unanswered? What about when our faith grows lukewarm? In these cases, we have the assurance and comfort of knowing we are chosen by God. God chose us to have an everlasting future.

God did this so that we might, among other things, "....proclaim the mighty acts of God..." How do we do that? I have two ideas. First, as the opportunity presents itself, share your faith with others, including your doubts and unanswered questions. Just be honest. The Holy Spirit will work through our words to create faith in others. Sometimes the response will be immediate and sometimes not, but be assured the Holy Spirit works through your words. Second, invite people to church. Many people who don't attend worship have at least thought about attending. The Holy Spirit will work through our invitation, sometimes immediately and sometimes over a period of years. Let's proclaim the mighty acts of God.

Written March 4, 2006

Resurrection

"But in fact Christ has been raised from the dead, the first fruits of those who have died."

I Corinthians 15:20

The Corinthian church was denying the reality of a bodily resurrection. St. Paul was writing to correct that view. He said that if we are not bodily raised, then Christ hasn't been raised either. Then comes the verse written above, "But in fact Christ has been raised..." Because Christ was bodily raised, we will be raised when he comes again. The resurrection of Jesus is the focal point of our faith. Everything hangs on it. Because Jesus lives, we worship. We don't go to church as an end in itself. We go because of Jesus. Because Jesus lives, we serve. Because Jesus lives, we have hope when there are no earthly grounds for it. Because Jesus lives, press on in worship, service, and in hope.

Written April 1, 2006

Fear to Hope

"The Lord is my light and my salvation; whom shall I fear? The Lord is the stronghold of my life; of whom shall I be afraid?"

Psalm 27:1

Each of us is afraid of something. It is different things for every one of us, but each of us is afraid of something. As the verse above makes clear, God strengthens us in the midst of our fears. We look first to the cross. At the cross, Jesus said, "My God, my God, why have you forsaken me?" Jesus experienced complete separation from God. Because Jesus experienced this separation, we don't have to experience it. Because Jesus said, "My God...why have you forsaken me?" we don't have to say that. In Jesus, God is always with us to strengthen us in the midst of things of which we are afraid. Then we look to the resurrection of Jesus. Because Jesus was raised, we have the certainty of eternal life with God. This is the big picture. In this big picture, we are ultimately going to be fine. This changes our perspective. Because we will ultimately be fine, the things of which we are afraid seem smaller. What happens when the things of which we are afraid occur? Then two factors come into play. The first is the big picture. Remember, we are ultimately going to be fine. The second factor is God, because of Jesus, is always with us to strengthen us. The God of the resurrection, which is God's supreme authority over all things, is always with us. Thanks be to God.

Written May 1, 2006

Public Officials

"First of all, then, I urge that supplications, prayers, intercessions, and thanksgivings be made for everyone, for kings and all who are in high positions, so that we may lead a quiet and peaceable life in all godliness and dignity."

1 Timothy 2:1-2

With the 4th of July coming in a few days, I thought these verses appropriate. One of our responsibilities is to pray for our public officials. A bit of history might be helpful. When these verses were written, the Roman Emperor demanded to be worshipped as a god and was persecuting Christians. Simultaneously, the writer asks the Christians to pray for the Emperor. We need to pray for our public officials, too. While a few officials are corrupt, most, in both parties, are honestly trying to do a good job. They also have a difficult job. They need our prayers. Let's pray for our public officials.

One aspect of these verses that struck me as I was studying them was the directive to be thankful for our public officials. Remember, when these verses were written, the Emperor was persecuting Christians. However, the writer asks Christians to give thanks for him. Let's also give thanks for our officials. Most of us have felt our blood pressure rise when our officials do something we view as abhorrent. I know the feeling. When we give thanks for our public officials, something wonderful happens. That is that our differences seem smaller. We have a greater appreciation for those officials with whom we disagree. Let's pray and give thanks for our public officials.

Written June 1, 2006

You Can Do It

"Therefore, since we are surrounded by so great a cloud of witnesses, let us also lay aside every weight and the sin that clings so closely, and let us run with perseverance the race that is set before us, looking to Jesus the pioneer and perfecter of our faith, who for the sake of the joy that was set before him endured the cross, disregarding its shame, and has taken his seat at the right hand of the throne of God."

Hebrews 12:1 & 2

When the writer proclaims, "Therefore, since we are surrounded by so great a cloud of witnesses…" a picture is painted for us. It is a picture of an athletic arena in which we are the runners. The people in the stands, i.e. "witnesses", are first the Old Testament people mentioned in the preceding chapter, and second those Christians who have lived the Christian faith and who have since died. They may be people who have died who were close to us. The "race that is set before us" symbolizes our living the Christian faith. As we strive to do so, it is as if the people in the stands are saying, "You can do it, You can do it, You can do it."

To run the race, we also need a leader we can follow. For this we have Jesus. For Jesus, the race included the cross. For the joy that was beyond the cross, Jesus faithfully ran the race. As we run our race of living the Christian faith, focus on Jesus. Sometimes we become discouraged. In that discouragement we say, "What's the use?" I know that discouragement personally. As we run the race, remember to focus on Jesus, and hear the people in the stands saying, "You can do it, You can do it, You can do it!"

Written July 1, 2006

The Reason We Were Created

"Make a joyful noise to the Lord, all the earth. Worship the Lord with gladness; Come into his presence with singing."

Psalm 100:1 & 2

We were created to praise God. When the Psalm writer said, "Make a joyful noise to the Lord...," we are asked to do what God created us to do. What about when we don't feel like praising God? Sometimes the circumstances of life are so overwhelmingly negative that we don't feel God deserves praise. I have been there. Let me tell you a personal story. For a long time, I didn't feel like praising God because of this illness. When I went to church, I hung on every word that asked God for something, but I spaced out on the Hymn of Praise and other songs that featured words of praise. I just didn't feel like praising God. After a period of personal introspection, I started focusing on the words to the Hymn of Praise and other hymns that praised God. I felt better after I did that. Why? It is because we were created for praising God.

This affects our motivation for worship. Our motivation for worship is vital. It's not so much what we get out of worship; it is what we put into it—in other words, praising God. The primary focus of worship is to praise God. It is what we were created to do.

Written August 1, 2006

Consolation

"Blessed be the God and Father of our Lord Jesus Christ, the Father of mercies and the God of all consolation, who consoles us in all our affliction, so that we maybe able to console those who are in any affliction with the consolation with which we ourselves are consoled by God."

2 Corinthians 1:3&4

It's no accident that these verses begin our funeral liturgy. They contain both the vertical and horizontal dimensions of our faith. The vertical dimension pertains to our relationship with God. God consoles us in this way. The cross is every sin, every tragedy, every misfortune, and ultimately our death. At the cross, Jesus assumed all of these things. In his resurrection he displayed his dominance over these aspects of our lives. It is as if Jesus is saying to us in every guilt and tragedy, "I have been there; these things will not last." We are consoled by this.

The horizontal dimension pertains to our relationship with each other. We can console each other too. Certainly we do this by our prayers. When we lift each other with our needs to God in prayer, God will answer. I believe we also share the presence of Christ and so console each other by listening. When we listen to each other in the midst of tragedy, we share their burdens. When we do this, their burdens become lighter. As we do this, we share the presence of Christ. Let's pray for each other. Let's listen to each other. Let's share the good news of Christ with each other.

Written September 1, 2006

Origins of Faith

"Then the disciples came to Jesus privately and said, 'Why could we not cast it out?' He said to them, 'Because of your little faith. For truly I tell you, if you have faith the size of a mustard seed, you will say to this mountain, "Move from here to there," and it will move, and nothing will be impossible for you.'"

Matthew 17:19-20

These verses are the climax of a story where a father brings his epileptic son to Jesus' disciples, petitioning them to heal the boy. They could not do so. When Jesus rejoins the disciples, he heals the boy. The disciples ask why they were unable to heal him. Jesus replies it was because of their lack of faith. Then come these verses.

Frequently these verses, and other verses pertaining to faith, are misunderstood. Often we think that we have to try harder to have more faith. We think if only I had more faith my, or my wife's, or my child's illness would be healed. We think if only I had more faith this tragedy would not have happened. This is a mistake. Faith comes from hearing about Christ. When Christ is proclaimed, the Holy Spirit creates faith within us. Faith doesn't come from trying harder. It comes from the proclamation of Christ. This is why worship is vital to faith. In worship, Christ is proclaimed. The Holy Spirit then works to create or strengthen faith within us. Faith won't prevent all tragedies, but it will draw us closer to God when tragedy happens. Let's hear Christ proclaimed and grow in faith.

Written October 1, 2006

Christmas Equals the Cross

"Surely he has borne our infirmities and carried our diseases; yet we accounted him stricken, struck down by God, and afflicted. But he was wounded for our transgressions, crushed for our iniquities; upon him was the punishment that made us whole, and by his bruises we are healed. All we like sheep have gone astray; we have all turned to our own way, and the Lord has laid on him the iniquity of us all."

Isaiah 53:4-6

This section of Isaiah features various passages regarding a suffering servant. The servant would undergo violent suffering on behalf of the people. We now know that servant was Jesus. These verses describe graphically the suffering of Jesus on our behalf. At the cross, Jesus absorbed our sin, thus forgiving us and freeing us from it. Jesus, at the cross, felt the weight of our diseases, loneliness, tragedies, and misfortunes. There is no sin, disease, or tragedy that Jesus did not feel on the cross. These verses portray that. That's why the cross is central to our faith.

We are about to commence our Christmas activities. I do not believe we can celebrate Jesus' birth without being mindful of the cross. The cross was Jesus' destiny. The cross will drive the harmful sentimentality out of Christmas. Christmas is busy for some, a rat race for a few, and a lonely time for many. Whatever state you find yourself in this December, look to the cross. The cross will give us a new perspective on our situation. If you find yourself too busy, that perspective will slow you down, tell you to do less, and see the needs of others. If you are lonely, you are not alone. Jesus is with you. If you are struggling with something, the cross will tell you that Jesus is on your side. As we celebrate Jesus' birth, look to the cross and gain a new perspective.

Written November 1, 2006

A New Beginning

"The steadfast love of the Lord never ceases, his mercies never come to an end; they are new every morning; great is your faithfulness. 'The Lord is my portion,' says my soul, 'therefore I will hope in him.'"

Lamentations 3:22-24

These verses are appropriate as we begin a new year. God's mercies are indeed new every morning. Some background on Lamentations perhaps might be helpful. Lamentations is a lament on the destruction of Jerusalem. Everything near and dear to the people was taken away. The author was extremely despondent. Yet, in this despondency, the author proclaims an eternal truth. That is that God's mercies are new every morning. That truth was fulfilled in Christ.

God's mercies for us are new every morning also. In baptism, we experience that mercy. In baptism, our sin is drowned. It is washed away. It is a new beginning for us. It is a new birth in Christ. We are born again. What happens when we repeatedly sin, as we all do? God renews our baptism every day. Every day we are reborn in Christ. We are literally born again, and again, and again. When the writer says about God's mercies that, "They are new every morning," it does not mean that a bad day will automatically be turned into a good one. Experience tells us that. What it does mean is that God daily renews our baptism and that God is with us no matter what comes. As we enter a new year, God's mercies are new every morning.

Written December 1, 2006

Patience Through Suffering

"In this you rejoice, even if now for a little while you have had to suffer various trials, so that the genuineness of your faith — being more precious than gold that, though perishable, is tested by fire — may be found to result in praise and glory, and honor, when Jesus Christ is revealed."

1 Peter 1:6-7

Jesus is coming again. We rejoice in this, as the verses above indicate. A month ago we celebrated his birth, when he came as a baby. He is coming again to save us. Sometimes the circumstances of life are overwhelming, and it seems like his coming is irrelevant. It may be an illness, job loss, the loss of a loved one, a divorce, or some other tragedy or suffering. These are overwhelming and make Jesus' coming seem irrelevant. When these things happen, we need to see the large picture. In the large picture these things, relatively speaking, are short lived when seen in the light of Jesus' coming. Jesus will come again to gather us to live with him forever. When seen in the light of forever, these problems are temporary.

I have said repeatedly that God does not cause tragedy or suffering. I firmly believe this. I also believe that God works through these things when they occur. God works to teach us patience. This is a difficult quality to learn. I have never been a patient person when it comes to health issues. Most of us would rather that God solve our problems than teach us patience. This has been a struggle for me. What God has taught me is that patience is necessary to discern what God is doing in my situation. With patience, we can each see what God is doing in our circumstance. That is why the confirmation prayer, when the confirmand is kneeling says "Give him/her patience in suffering." With patience we can see what God is doing in our lives, help those who need help, and be ready when Jesus comes to save us all.

Written January 1, 2007

God's Kingdom is Near

"Now after John was arrested, Jesus came to Galilee, proclaiming the good news of God, and saying, 'The time is fulfilled, and the kingdom of God has come near; repent, and believe in the good news.'"

Mark 1:14-15

There are two aspects of these verses about which I want to write. One is that the kingdom of God is near; the other is Jesus' call to repent. When Jesus said, "The kingdom of God has come near," he brought the kingdom of God to us. We live in the kingdom of God today. Sometimes it doesn't seem like it. With sin, war, poverty, illness, abuse, and oppression, it seems like the kingdom of God is light years away. We live in two realities. One is the maladies listed. The other is that Jesus brought the kingdom of God to us. We live in the kingdom of God. It is indeed near. It will be fulfilled in the age to come, but is present now. We have every reason to be optimistic and hopeful as we help those who need help, work for justice and peace, and share our faith. The kingdom of God is near. Jesus brought it.

Jesus also called us to repent. That is, Jesus called us to turn our lives around. We do this, not to bring God's kingdom, but because God's kingdom has come. This is an on-going process. We don't just repent once. We do it all the time. We do it every time we make a decision or set a priority. What about when we don't want to change? What about when we like things the way they are? You and I struggle with this constantly. My advice is look to the cross. Jesus died for everything that needs changing. Jesus died for everything that needs changing in your life and in mine. Look to the cross and repent. Look to the cross and turn things around. Repent because the kingdom of God has come.

Written February 1, 2007

The Reality of Sin

"...My God, my God, why have you forsaken me?"

Matthew 27:46

These are Jesus' words from the cross. There are two things I want to write about them. The first is that we often don't take sin seriously enough; the other is that we often live with guilt. In terms of sin, we often deny it. When we sin, we sometimes say, "I just made a mistake." Or we might go as far as saying, "I cut corners." Sin separates us from God. When Jesus said, "My God, my God, why have you forsaken me," he was carrying your sin and mine. At that point, he was separated from God because he was carrying our sin. That's what sin does – it separates us from God. The next time you or I tend to deny our sin, let's hear the words of Jesus from the cross. Our sin separates us from God. We can see that in Jesus.

The other truth is that we often live with guilt. An example of that is when we confess the same sin over and over again. We don't need to do that. Because Jesus carried our sins, we don't have to carry them ourselves. That is the meaning of forgiveness. As baptized people, we live as God's forgiven people. This doesn't mean we don't sin. It does mean that Jesus carried our sins to the cross and was separated from God on our behalf. Sometimes today we live by the slogan, "If something seems too good to be true, it is." While that line is true in some circumstances, it is not true with God. Jesus carried our sin so we don't have to. The next time we hear Jesus' words, "My God, my God, why have you forsaken me," let's say thanks be to God.

Written March 1, 2007

Steadfastness

"Therefore, my beloved, be steadfast, immovable, always excelling in the work of the Lord, because you know that in the Lord your labor is not in vain."

1 Corinthians 15:58

1 Corinthians 15 is the most complete chapter in the Bible on what Jesus' resurrection means to us. I encourage you to read it in its entirety. Among other things, it says that because Jesus was bodily raised our sins are forgiven. Frequently, we have difficulty with this. We think we need to do something to earn God's forgiveness. Hear what the resurrection means for our forgiveness. Because Jesus was bodily raised, we don't need to do something. Because Jesus was bodily raised, it's a done deal— our sins are forgiven. We don't need to live with guilt; just thank God. The chapter also says that because Jesus was raised, our bodies will be raised when Jesus comes again. We have problems and difficulties in this life. We also have a future with God. As Jesus was bodily raised, we will be raised also. As other scripture indicates, those problems and difficulties will be gone. This also is a done deal.

Because of these facts, St. Paul concludes the chapter with the triumphant verse written above. "Know that in the Lord your labor is not in vain." We sometimes become discouraged in our Christian service. We don't see results, and we become physically tired. We burn out. The key is prayer. If we are prayerfully doing what God wants us to do, all will be fine. Remember, we serve a living Lord, who was bodily raised. We may or may not see results of our service. The Holy Spirit will take care of results in due time. If you pray about the things you do, "Know that in the Lord your labor is not in vain." This is because we serve a living Lord.

Written April 1, 2007

Testing Our Faith

"No testing has overtaken you that is not common to everyone. God is faithful, and he will not let you be tested beyond your strength, but with the testing he will also provide the way out so that you may be able to endure it."

1 Corinthians 10:13

This verse is often misinterpreted with the line, "God won't give you more than you can handle." This is a tragic misinterpretation. One, God doesn't give bad things; and two, some people do get more than they can handle. Paul wrote these lines to encourage us. Previously in this chapter, Paul cites occasions where God's Old Testament people had their faith tested by their circumstances in life. Frequently, they failed and found themselves separated from God. Paul writes these lines to strengthen us when our faith is tested.

Often the circumstances of life test our faith. This illness has tested mine. Frequently I have asked, "Where is God in this?" or "Why doesn't God heal me?" Your faith has been tested too, or will be tested. It may or may not be an illness, but the circumstances of life test all of us sooner or later. All of us will find our faith tested. That is why Paul wrote these lines. As Paul says, "God...will provide a way out." God does this in many ways. There are two I would like to write about. One is worship; the other is prayer. We worship, not only because it is appropriate, but, quite frankly, because it strengthens our faith when we are tested. Worship provides a foundation of faith before we are tested; and strengthens us when we are. I don't know where my faith would be if I were not able to attend worship. God also provides a way out through prayer. When we pray for ourselves and others, God strengthens us. In a mystery, we may not obtain the answers we desire, but God strengthens us. I can attest to that. Through worship and prayer, God provides a way out when our faith is tested. That inevitably happens.

Written May 1, 2007

Hope in Clay Jars

"But we have this treasure in clay jars, so that it may be made clear that this extraordinary power belongs to God and does not come from us. We are afflicted in every way, but not crushed; perplexed, but not driven to despair; persecuted, but not forsaken; struck down, but not destroyed;"

2 Corinthians 4:7-9

In verse 7 there are three operative words: "Treasure," "Clay jars", and "Power." The treasure is the gospel of Christ. When we sin, Jesus brings forgiveness. When we are in despair, Jesus brings hope. When we fear, Jesus brings assurance. When we fail, Jesus brings a second chance. When we die, Jesus brings resurrection. This is the treasure we have in the gospel of Christ. It is good news.

We have this treasure in clay jars. Paul uses "clay jars" to describe him and us. That's not very flattering. We sin. We are vulnerable to disease, despair, hopelessness, failure, and fear. We die. Such is our condition without the treasure of the gospel of Christ.

In verses 8 and 9 we see the results of God's power through Christ. Paul describes various afflictions that he and other Christians have experienced. We experience them too. This is a reality. Being a Christian does not make us immune to these things. Paul, however, is not defeated by them. Neither are we. Why is this so? It is because of the resurrection of Christ. At the cross, Jesus felt all these things and died. Then God raised him. We share in that victory. That is why we are not defeated. Our baptism unites us in this victory of Christ. That is why we experience affliction, but are not defeated. The resurrection of Christ displays the power of God. By our baptism and faith, we share in that power.

Written June 1, 2007

Our Need for Jesus

Jesus answered,"Those who are well have no need of a physician, but those who are sick; I have come to call not the righteous but sinners to repentance."

Luke 5: 31-32

Jesus had just called Levi (Matthew) to be one of his disciples. Levi, because of his occupation as a tax collector, was considered a social outcast. He threw a banquet for Jesus. At the banquet were other social outcasts. Jesus was criticized for associating with such people. His response to the criticism was the verses written above. Jesus describes himself as a physician who can heal.

We all need Jesus. All of us sin and need his forgiveness. We all need to repent, that is, turn around from sin. We do this constantly decision by decision, priority by priority.

Jesus is a physician for other things also. It may be that we need healing in personal relationships. It may be that a long standing personal grudge needs to be forgiven. It may be for a new direction in life. It may be for hope in the midst of illness or in the midst of the mundane drudgery of life. It may be other things for you. My advice to you is to pray and seek answers to whatever is bothering you. Jesus will answer. He will heal you with peace. Jesus promised to help. We all need Jesus.

Written July 1, 2007

The Silence of God

"How long, O Lord? Will you forget me forever? How long will you hide your face from me? I will sing to the Lord, because he has dealt bountifully with me."

Psalms 13:1, 6

Psalm 13, like many Psalms, is a lament. The writer is feeling forgotten by God in the midst of personal problems. The writer is experiencing God's silence. That is painful. We experience God's silence also. In personal problems and the world's problems, we often experience God's silence. We wonder why God doesn't do something. This is frustrating as well as painful. We would rather God speak and act.

Why is God sometimes silent? I believe it is because it forces us to look at ourselves. Though it can be painful, it forces us to see how completely and utterly dependent on God we are. When we realize that, we pray and worship more. When we do that, we grow in faith. This lifts us up. I believe there is another reason why God is occasionally silent. It is because it causes us to look at the needs of our neighbors both near and far. When we do that, we become more sensitive to their needs and try to meet them. All in all, God's silence leads us to grow in faith and action. As C.S. Lewis inferred, God screams at us through the silence. This lifts us to praise God. This caused the Psalm writer to conclude that lament with the following words, "I will sing to the Lord, because he has dealt bountifully with me."

Written August 1, 2007

The Means of Grace

"Ho, everyone who thirsts, come to the waters; and you that have no money, come, buy and eat! Come, buy wine and milk without money and without price. Why do you spend your money for that which is not bread and your labor for that which does not satisfy? Listen carefully to me, and eat what is good, and delight yourselves in rich food."

Isaiah 55:1&2

This is a metaphor for God's grace, restoration, and redemption. God's grace comes in many ways. It comes when we worship. In worship, we hear God's word and receive the sacraments. These are the means of grace today. God's grace comes in words of encouragement and support from others. The reason we were created is to be recipients of God's grace. That is the reason we are alive. God's grace will give us meaning in the midst of life's problems. In my case, when illness occurs, it is an anchor in the stormy seas of life. "And you who have no money, come, buy and eat." That is God's grace. This is why we were created.

Verse 2 is a metaphor for our human condition. It says we often settle for less than God's grace. That is our human condition. In life we constantly struggle with this. It will be different things for each of us, but the tendency is to settle for less than what God created us to be. It's like the story of the little boy who waited for the circus to come to his town. When the circus arrived, with great joy he went. At the circus there were side shows. Each said, "Come here and win." Of course he did, but he didn't win. He became so involved with the side shows that he missed the main event. The main event in life is God's grace. Let's not miss it. It's the reason for which we were created.

Written September 1, 2007

Closer to Jesus

"Then one of them, when he saw that he was healed, turned back, praising God with a loud voice. He prostrated himself at Jesus' feet and thanked him. And he was a Samaritan."

Luke 17:15 & 16

These verses represent the climax of the story in which ten lepers were healed. The story runs from verse 11 through verse 19; I encourage you to read it. All ten lepers were healed, but only one returned to thank Jesus. The nine who did not return to give thanks can hardly be faulted in that they were doing what Jesus asked them to do. Though, as the story makes clear, Jesus wished they had all returned to give thanks. One thing is clear. The one who thanked Jesus enhanced his relationship with Jesus.

It works that way for us also. Thanking Jesus edifies our relationship with him. Jesus has given us eternal life and the forgiveness of our sins. Thank Jesus for these gifts. Even with these gifts, life can be bleak, as this illness has taught me. What I have learned from this illness, or more accurately what God has taught me, is to find little things in the midst of the bleakness for which to give thanks. It may be simply God getting us through the day or a positive answer to a prayer. Thank Jesus for these things, however small they seem to be.

We also need to look at the identity of the Samaritan. He was considered an outcast among God's people. Had he done what Jesus asked him to do, he probably would have received a cold shoulder from the priests. Maybe we feel we have received a cold shoulder from life. I suppose we all feel that way at times. When we feel that way, we have Jesus. He meets us with eternal life, forgiveness, and acceptance. Thank him for these gifts. Thankfulness enlivens our relationship with Jesus.

Written October 1, 2007

Pray Without Ceasing

"Pray without ceasing."

1 Thessalonians 5:17

This verse was written as Paul instructed the people on how to live as they awaited the second coming of Christ. This message is vital for us also. "Pray without ceasing" is a message for us as we await the coming of Christ – both as a baby and his triumphant second coming. This illness has taught me things about prayer. First, whether or not we obtain the answers we desire, prayer deepens our relationship with God. Think about personal friendships. If we communicate regularly with them, the relationship becomes closer. If we don't, the relationship becomes distant. It's the same way with God. Prayer is communication with God. Through a mystery, prayer deepens our relationship with God whether we receive the desired answers or not. For example, I have prayed for physical healing. To this date that has not happened; yet, during this illness, I have grown in Christ and my relationship with God has deepened.

Second, while it is important to pray for ourselves, it is equally important to pray for others and the world situation. They need our prayers and we need to pray for them. If we only pray for ourselves, our relationship with God becomes insular and self centered. To the extent we pray for others, we are drawn outward. This is healthy for us.

Third, it is vital that we thank God for things, however small. We may need to think of things for which to be thankful, but when we do, we realize how good God is. Thank God for good things.

As we prepare to enter December, it will be a busy month for many and a lonely time for some. Take time during December for prayer. It will provide the serenity that comes from a deeper relationship with God. It will prepare us for Jesus' coming.

Written November 1, 2007

Raised with Christ

"For through the law I died to the law, so that I might live to God. I have been crucified with Christ; and it is no longer I who live, but it is Christ who lives in me. And the life I now live in the flesh I live by faith in the Son of God who loved me and gave himself for me."

Galations 2:19 & 20

God's law (what God tells us to do and not to do) kills us. The reason it does so is that we are incapable of perfectly obeying God's law. That is why Paul says, "I have been crucified with Christ." In baptism we are united with Christ. That means as Christ died, so do we. We die to the belief that we can obey God on our own. As we spiritually renew our baptism daily, we die to this belief every day. Then, what becomes of obedience? We obey because we love Christ. In baptism we are not only united with Christ in death; we are united with him in resurrection. As Jesus was raised, and as we daily renew our baptism, daily we are raised to follow him in loving obedience. For us, the future is exclusively positive. As Jesus was raised and daily we are raised with him, we have forgiveness and everlasting life. We obey not on our own, but because in love for Christ we can't help it.

Written December 1, 2007

My Yoke is Easy

"Come to me, all you that are weary and are carrying heavy burdens, and I will give you rest. Take my yoke upon you, and learn from me; for I am gentle and humble in heart, and you will find rest for your souls. For my yoke is easy, and my burden is light."

Matthew 11:28-30

Jesus invites you who are weary to come to him. Life can be wearisome at times. The causes of this are many. It may be the stress of trying to meet the expectations of others or our own expectations. It may be illness, experienced personally or by a loved one. It may be something else for you. Whatever the cause, Jesus invites us to come to him. Obviously, being a Christian will not preclude problems; but Jesus will give us peace in the midst of those problems.

Jesus said, "My yoke is easy." The implications are apparent. When an animal was yoked, it was for work. We are to work for Jesus. Jesus says there is peace in this. You may be thinking, I am already stressed with church work. How can there be peace in this? The key is prayer. God will guide you in what you are supposed to do. In regard to church work, some are too busy while others aren't busy enough. This applies to life in general also. The key is prayer. God will guide you in what you should drop from your schedule and guide you in what you should add. If we are doing what God wants us to do, it is true that Jesus' "Yoke is easy."

Written January 1, 2008

The Value of Trust

"*Even youths will faint and be weary, and the young will fall exhausted; but those who wait for the Lord shall renew their strength, they shall mount up with wings like eagles, they shall run and not be weary, they shall walk and not faint.*"

Isaiah 40:30-31

Trust God no matter what happens. That is the message of these verses. When it says "Wait upon the Lord," it connotes trust. Trust in God no matter what happens. Perhaps a bit of history on these verses will be helpful. God's people had been in captivity for a generation. Most of them wanted to return to their homeland. People were born and they died without hope. Though Isaiah, Chapter 40, proclaims God is about to act, I suspect that many found their sense of trust waning. God did act and released the people. All they had to do was trust. It's the same for us. In our age, wars rage and conflicts abound. Yet, God will see us through. All God asks is that we trust.

Trust doesn't preclude other feelings we may have about God. Sometimes we are angry at God. Sometimes we are disappointed in God. Sometimes we are dismayed with God. I suppose we all have these feelings at one time or another. Under girding these feelings there still remains trust in God. This is important. If trust remains, we can share these feelings with God and Christian friends and, thus, resolve these feelings. In baptism, we were born as God's children. God won't give up on us. God will see us through. God, who is revealed in Jesus, is trustworthy. Trust God no matter what happens.

Written February 1, 2008

God With Us

"Therefore the Lord himself will give you a sign. Look, the young woman is with child and shall bear a son, and shall name him Immanuel."

Isaiah 7:14

This verse is often used in the weeks prior to Christmas, but is applicable all year long. God's people were threatened militarily and, as a sign of God's presence, a young woman will have a son and his name will be called Immanuel. Immanuel means "God with us." God was with them. God is with us also. While this verse has various Old Testament meanings, it was ultimately fulfilled in Jesus. In Jesus, God is with us. I confess that I have had problems with this. I not only want God to be with me; I want God to do something dramatic. Probably most of us have felt this way from time to time. I have asked, "Why doesn't God heal my illness?" You may have asked, "Why doesn't God heal my wife's, or husband's illness?" "Why didn't God prevent that accident?" "Why doesn't God do something dramatic with this problem I have?" What I have painfully learned through this illness is that things don't work that way. Often God doesn't work in the dramatic way that we wish God would work. Instead we can learn from the church year, a portion of which we have just gone through. The cross is God's embrace of us in the midst of our problems. God is not only with us; God is carrying us. The resurrection is God's answer to our problems. Our problems don't have the final say. God does. Through the resurrection, we are made God's people forever. God is indeed with us.

Written March 1, 2008

Forgiveness

"As far as the east is from the west, so far he removes our transgressions from us."

Psalm 103:12

Praise God. This is God's promise to us. The penalty for sin (transgressions) is complete separation from God. That's why the cross is central to our faith. When Jesus moaned from the cross, "My God, my God, why have you forsaken me," he was experiencing that separation so that we wouldn't have to. In his resurrection he guarantees forgiveness. We don't have to live with guilt. We are forgiven. Praise God.

What should we do with this forgiveness? First, thank and praise God. This is what we were created to do. The dynamics of thankfulness are amazing. The dynamics are such that the more we give thanks for forgiveness and other things that God has done, the more we realize what God has done. Second, repent. Repentance means to turn one's life around. We do this day by day, decision by decision, priority by priority. Forgiveness comes first. We respond by turning our lives around. Third, make amends to people we have wronged. Alcoholics Anonymous has as one of its steps to make amends with people they have wronged, except when to do so would cause harm. This is good advice for all of us. We don't fully appreciate God's forgiveness until we make amends to people we have wronged. If making amends would cause harm to people, just accept God's forgiveness and be thankful for it. We are forgiven. Praise God.

Written April 1, 2008

Thankfulness in all Circumstances

"Give thanks in all circumstances; for this is the will of God in Christ Jesus for you."

1 Thessalonians 5:18

There are some things for which it is easy to be thankful— a good day, a beautiful outdoor scene, or when things go the way we desire. There are other circumstances in which thankfulness is difficult, if not impossible. Note that the verse says, "Be thankful 'in' all circumstances." It does not say be thankful "for" all circumstances. That's a big difference. The background of 1st Thessalonians 5 is the second coming of Jesus. Because Jesus is coming again, the people were to be thankful. So are we. Think of who you are. Jesus made you his people in baptism. He is coming again to make us his people forever. That is why we can be thankful in all circumstances. We are God's people—forever.

In a bit of irony, I believe suffering increases our thankfulness. I didn't ask for this illness, and I would get rid of it yesterday if I could, but it has made me more thankful for my relationship with God. I am thankful for things that I formerly took for granted. Here is what has been helpful for me. Think of things, however small, for which to be thankful. When you do that, you realize how God is providing for you. When you do that, it magnifies that you are a child of God. Because we are God's people, we can be thankful in, not for, all circumstances.

Written May 1, 2008

Thankfulness for People

"I thank my God every time I remember you, constantly praying with joy in every one of my prayers for all of you."

Philippians 1:3-4

Paul, the author of Philippians, was very thankful for the Philippian congregation. I am very thankful for you, the people of Bethlehem. Through some rough times when my faith was challenged through my illness, you kept my faith going and strong. It was by your presence in worship. The dynamics of worship are as follows. When we come together for worship, Christ is proclaimed. The Holy Spirit works through that proclamation to strengthen our faith. All of us have our faith challenged at one time or another. It is important that we be in worship so that the Holy Spirit can strengthen our faith. The key is that we come together to hear the proclamation of Christ. Thank you for your presence in worship. You have strengthened my faith by being there. Many of you have joined Bethlehem since I was a pastor there, thus I do not know you personally. However, I recognize faces. Whether I know you or not, I miss you when you are not there. Thank you for your presence in worship. Through your presence in worship, you have kept my faith going and strong. I am thankful for that. I am thankful for you.

Written June 1, 2008

Be Like a Child

"At that time the disciples came to Jesus and asked, 'Who is the greatest in the kingdom of heaven?' He called a child, whom he put among them, and said, 'Truly I tell you, unless you change and become like children, you will never enter the kingdom of heaven. Whoever becomes humble like this child is the greatest in the kingdom of heaven. Whoever welcomes one such child in my name welcomes me.'"

Matthew 18:1-5

The disciples were concerned about greatness. In answer to their question, Jesus put a child in their midst and said, "Be like this child." In that culture, children had little rights. They were totally dependent on their parents. In the same way, we are totally dependent on God. In fact, we are dependent on God for our next breath. Luther said, "God is God because God creates." If someone else created, that someone would be God. Creation isn't a one time event. Creation is on-going. For example, we are dependent on God to create our next breath. That is how dependent on God we are. Also, we are dependent on God for our forgiveness and eternal life. We need to be thankful for that dependence, because God is, quite frankly, dependable. Thank God for our dependence.

What about when bad things happen? I have said repeatedly that God does not cause bad things to happen; however, they obviously do happen. What do we do when we have done everything we can and the problem persists? Jesus told us. Like a little child, depend on God in faith. God will see us through. Applying this personally, I have repeatedly prayed for God's healing. To this date, that has not happened. That has made me very frustrated. What do I do in this frustration? Look in faith to God. Whatever the outcome of this illness, God will see me through. Such is our dependence on God. Thank God for that dependence. God will see us through. Whatever the circumstance, look in faith to our ideal heavenly parent.

Written July 1, 2008

Hope Through Suffering

"Therefore, since we are justified by faith, we have peace with God through our Lord Jesus Christ, through whom we have obtained access to this grace in which we stand; and we boast in our hope of sharing the glory of God. And not only that, but we also boast in our sufferings, knowing that suffering produces endurance, and endurance produces character, and character produces hope, and hope does not disappoint us, because God's love has been poured into our hearts through the Holy Spirit that has been given to us."

Romans 5:1-5

We have peace with God. Every sin which destroys that peace is forgiven through Jesus. Our relationship with God is the most important possession we have. It gives us purpose for living. While we need other things also, our relationship with God is the most important. Without a relationship with God, we will resort to other things to achieve satisfaction. They are things which ultimately will fail us. With a relationship with God, we are able to keep going when everything else is taken away. Thank God for peace with God.

What about when bad things happen? Though God does not cause bad things or suffering, they happen to most of us at one time or another. In an ironic twist, I believe that suffering increases hope. The logical thing is to get angry with God when suffering initially occurs. I sure did. However, over time suffering increases hope. After thirteen years of this illness, I have more hope in God than I ever did before this illness occurred. How can we be sure of this hope? It is because of the Holy Spirit. The Holy Spirit is God working in our lives. We receive the Holy Spirit in baptism. As certainly as we were baptized, the Holy Spirit is working in our lives to give us hope in the midst of suffering. It may take time and resolution of our anger, but the Holy Spirit works through suffering to give us hope. Thank God for peace. Thank God for hope. Thank the Holy Spirit.

Written August 1, 2008

Why are you cast down, O my soul, and why are you disquieted within me? Hope in God; for I shall again praise him, my help and my God.

Psalms 42:11

When 'In Sickness and Health' Became a Reality

By Bonnie L. Roberts

I was born into a loving Christian home. My mom and dad were a shining example of dedication and love for each other. I had an older sister, Janie, and an older brother, Gary. We were raised on a dairy farm near Mora, MN. Being raised in a farming community, our family worked together. I learned how to work and make things work. (I had no idea how that would come into play later in my life.) We spent lots of time together baling hay, milking cows, and working the fields. Janie, Gary, and I still chuckle together that our idea of fun was working together! I really feel that there is a special bond between us all because of the farming community atmosphere.

I met the love of my life when I was 18 years old. My brother, Gary, led to become a pastor, was attending Northwestern Seminary in St. Paul. Our family wanted to celebrate his birthday with him. So, on a Sunday noon, we drove down to a restaurant in the cities to meet him and a friend of his from seminary. That friend turned out to be my future husband, Don. I don't believe in love at first sight, but I did think he was a very special guy from the moment I met him.

We started dating during my college years at St. Cloud State University. When his seminary internship in Babylon, NY separated us for a year, I wondered if we could maintain our relationship long distance. There were lots of letters, phone calls, and a trip to New York City for me. He returned in August 1974, and we were engaged to be married in November.

1975 was a very busy year for us. We were married one week, Don graduated from seminary the next, and one month later "the newlyweds" began their first parish ministry in St. James, MN. To this day, Don and I wonder how those loving people at East and West Sveadahl put up with us! Here we were newly married and thrust into the ministry as pastor and wife.

Let me thank those dear people for being patient and so kind to us for those three years. They were wonderful to us.

1978 brought us to Red Wing, MN to First Lutheran Church. These were some very special years for Don and myself. First Lutheran is an awesome congregation and we have many wonderful friends that we cherish to this day. Our children, Jeremy, Paul, and Katie were born in Red Wing, and began their growing up years there. Red Wing holds a very special place in my heart.

1989 brought us to our current congregation, Bethlehem Lutheran in Mankato. Don thoroughly enjoyed his ministry here. I always enjoyed being Don's shadow. By that I mean I

sang in the choir and used the talents God has given me, but as for public speaking and all that goes with it, I was very content to let Don use the talent God had given him. Don had a gift for preaching. I just wanted to support my husband.

Donald and Bonnie Roberts family
L-R: Donald holding Katie (age 3), Bonnie with Paul in front (age 7) and Jeremy (age 9) Taken at a farewell reception at 1ˢᵗ Lutheran Church in Red Wing, MN, November, 1989.

Our lives were flowing along very nicely. We were enjoying our life here; our children were enjoying the community of Mankato, growing up, and doing well. Then, in the spring of 1995, Don told me of some unusual symptoms in his fingers. I was shocked that he was thinking ALS at that point. By fall, he was diagnosed both here in Mankato, and then later at Mayo Clinic.

Both of our lives changed dramatically at that point. I had always heard the word "devastating disease" when describing ALS, and it is true. My heart was broken. We had no idea what we would have to face at that point or how bad things were going to get. My thoughts raced as to all the possible outcomes. We knew there were different forms of ALS with different severities. My faith in God helped me hang on at that time. One thing Don and I knew. What ever we had to face, we were going to meet head on together. After 20 years of a rock solid Christ centered marriage, now our feet hit the road living out the promises we made to each other on our wedding day.

The first five years of ALS progressed slowly for Don. I and our children managed to help Don with whatever was difficult for him, and we received help from my dear mom, Eunice. Church members also were a great help.

Our lives dramatically changed again on May 3, 2000, when Don required a ventilator to breathe. I knew then that I would not be able to handle our situation alone. Don and I had decided that we wanted to deal with ALS living together, or not at all. This would mean that we would need nursing care in our home for him. Home care, to the degree that we wanted it, was not easy to come by. We were in the hospital waiting for the availability of enough home care workers for almost 2 months. I remember our doctor and the hospital social worker's conversation with me, telling me it just wasn't going to work. We would have to use a facility far from our home. I cried uncontrollably that day. I wondered if they were right. I asked the Lord to reveal His will for us. Within a week, a home care provider came up with enough staff to send us home. I thank God for working it out for us.

The last seven years God has enabled Don and me to be together, living in our home. I have often wondered why God took Don out of parish ministry, only to see that for now He has called him into a much different kind of ministry, through the people he has ministered to right here in our home. He has changed so many lives of people who we would not have met

Donald and Bonnie Roberts
(taken at Lori Steen's wedding
on September 8, 2007)

had Don not become ill with ALS. I have seen God work through Don. Though every ounce of my being wants the illness to leave Don this very second, I know God is in complete control of our situation, and we entrust our lives to Him. Don and I continue to trust God for our needs, wants, and desires.

I don't want to mislead anyone going through a similar situation. We have our good and bad days with this illness. Don's limitations often bring sadness to my heart. I long to hear his voice again, and enjoy his special hugs. I try not to be overwhelmed when I see another couple doing the things that Don and I would give anything to enjoy again. At the beginning of Don's illness, I did go through a period when I felt angry at God for allowing this to happen to us. Now, I have gone full circle and feel God's presence in every part of my life, from my morning walk enjoying the fresh summer air to a late evening talk with one of my children. I am thankful to God for sustaining me through this and for the little things that bring joy to my day.

At one of my physicals at the beginning of Don's illness, my doctor, who was very sympathetic and supportive told me, "Bonnie, remember this is a marathon experience, not a sprint." Care giving can be very exhausting. Sometimes you have no emotional or physical energy left. Whenever a nurse cannot make a shift, I fill in. I have learned to take good care of myself. I watch my exercise, eating habits, and spiritual renewal. It is so easy to overextend yourself until you have nothing left. One of the nicest compliments anyone has given me came from my sister, Janie. She said, "Bonnie, you have made an impossible situation, possible." I know that it isn't me that makes our situation work. I know it is the presence of Christ and the strength he gives each one in our family to carry on each day. Thanks be to God that He makes the impossible, possible.

Finally, if I can encourage anyone whose loved one is going through something tough, don't give up. Lean on the Lord. His arms are wide and will enfold you in His love. He will give you new eyes to see things in a new way. Give Him complete control of every part of your life, and then watch Him work. You will be surprised what He will do. In whatever situation you find yourself today, I pray you will know God's peace in a special way and receive God's richest blessings.

Trip to the North Shore of Lake Superior, August, 2006.
L-R: Ruth, Don, Jeremy, and Bonnie Roberts and Eunice Schulz

Living With ALS - A Daughter's Perspective

"I know God will not give me anything I can't handle. I just wish that He didn't trust me so much."

Mother Teresa (1910-1997)

By Katie Jean Roberts

Despite the situation our family has been placed in, I feel I have the best parents anyone could ask for. Although I do wish that things would have been different, and that my dad wouldn't

Katie, Donald and Bonnie Roberts, taken on the day of Katie's college graduation, May 2008.

have been sick, I know my parents did the best they could for my brothers and I, which was more than I could ask for.

My mom has been amazing these past 12 years. Her strength and courage continues to impress me each day. Not only is she constantly taking care of my brothers and I, she is taking care of my dad as well. Day in and day out she has supported him, cared for him, and loved him. I only hope to be half the person she is someday.

My dad has always been there for me whenever I needed support or someone to talk to, even though he is probably the one who needs my support. He is always concerned about me. He is the one to always tell me to put my seat belt on, drive carefully when I leave the house, and remind me to get an oil change in my car every 3 months. In many ways, he is a typical father looking out for his daughter. That is the way I have always seen him. Every once in a while I stumble across a letter or note to my dad saying how he has changed someone's life through his faith and courage. I can't help but be proud of that. To go through everything that my father has, and come out the other end with a renewed faith in God, is something that I don't think many people can claim. It makes me extremely honored to be his daughter.

My own faith has gone through its own ups and downs as well in the past ten years. Yet, the thing that has gotten me through is the belief that God will never give me more than I can handle. I truly believe that the reason my family has gone through everything it has, is because God knew my dad and the rest of us could come out the other side okay, and so far we have.

The Roberts family at the ALS Walk in Mankato, MN, April 2008.
L-R: Eunice Schulz, Bonnie Roberts, Paul Roberts, Don Roberts,
Katie Roberts, Jeremy Roberts, Ethan Roberts in stroller,
Dawn Roberts, Will Sordahl, Carrie Roberts.